CW00471956

# THE REBORN DIVA

# The Reborn Diva

Marjorie Wright

JANUS PUBLISHING COMPANY LTD
Cambridge, England

First published in Great Britain 2016
by Janus Publishing Company Ltd
The Studio
High Green
Great Shelford
Cambridge CB22 5EG

www.januspublishing.co.uk

Copyright © Marjorie Wright 2016
British Library Cataloguing-in-Publication Data
A catalogue record for this book is available from the British Library

ISBN  978-1-85756-851-6

All rights reserved. No part of this publication may be reproduced,
stored in a retrieval system or transmitted in any form or by any
means, electric, mechanical, photocopying, recording or otherwise,
without the prior permission of the publisher.

The right of Marjorie Wright to be identified as the author
of this work has been asserted by her in accordance with the
Copyright, Designs and Patents Act 1988.

Cover Picture supplied by the Author

Cover Design: Janus Publishing Company Ltd

Printed and bound in the UK by PublishPoint
from KnowledgePoint Limited, Reading

To the People of Northern Ireland

# Contents

# Overture

'Marge, when you are happy you tell everyone, and boy, do you suffer for it.' How those words were to haunt me when my life changed for ever after the publication of my autobiography, *The Rise and Fall of a La Scala Diva*, which caused unimaginable turmoil after it revealed my celebrity lifestyle. And so, encouraged by cries of 'but one couldn't write the script; it's unbelievable', I shall try to tell you what happened to me – a gregarious, fun-loving musician – so that no other human being should be forced to experience the relentless mental torture and persecution I endured, all because God gave me a voice with which to entertain and make others happy.

Although I had left Ulster well before the Troubles began, my parents remained there throughout those terrible years of suffering, as they, like so many stoic and courageous people, refused to be driven out of their own country by thugs. Without meaning to date myself, may I explain that I am an 'afterthought' of an 'afterthought', and take great pride in my family role as the 'baby' of my generation of clannish Wrights. My arrival was a great a shock to my parents, as my father's was to my grandparents, who already had ten children of their own, as well as two from my grandfather's first marriage. And so, having survived two world wars and bloody Irish atrocities, including constant reminders of the Battle of the Boyne in 1690, they were well used to dealing with conflict.

By the time the civil war in Ulster had taken hold I was already settled in beautiful Rome, enjoying the end of the *dolce vita* era, when everyone lived life to the full, enjoying Italian wine and food, whether it be by the sea or just cooling off by the side of friends' swimming pools. To afford such a luxurious lifestyle I earned my living by deputising for indisposed, or deposed, sopranos, before eventually making my own mark on the international circuit. From the day I arrived in Rome for a sabbatical year on the Feast of the Epiphany not only did I fall in love with its extraordinary beauty and history but with the wonderfully kind and loving arms of those who embraced me, welcomed me into their homes and gave me unimaginable opportunities to believe in myself as a solo singer. I shall be eternally grateful to all those unselfish well-connected Italian administrators, conductors and composers who chose me to perform wonderful music in world-class venues, unearthing musical qualities within me of which even I was unaware. If I had known what was to be in store for my family and friends back home in Northern Ireland for the subsequent thirty years I might not have been so eager to abandon London for pastures new. On the other hand: how could I have imagined that a year 'away from it all' could have multiplied into fifteen, before dirty politics intervened to put a temporary halt to it all.

For those of us living abroad during the Troubles, coming from Ulster wasn't easy, especially for those of us with Belfast stamped on our passport as our place of birth. My fellow musicians and I were continuously eyed with suspicion and scrutinised by officials before we were finally allowed to pass through passport controls – once they had thumbed their way through their lists of suspects. I had to exchange my Irish passport for a British one after Swiss Customs boarded the train on which I was travelling from Stuttgart – the headquarters of the Baader-Meinhof Group – to Milan, where a policeman had been shot earlier that same day. If it hadn't been for the intervention of heroic fellow Italian passengers I would have been thrown off the train, which fortunately continued its journey with me still on board. Another colleague, who happened to play in a world-famous orchestra, was separated from his fellow musicians and interrogated, before he was freed to join them at the other side of passport control. When I was frequently asked if I was a Protestant or a Catholic I would leave my inquisitors in an even more baffled state by declaring that I was a Christian.

I grew up in the beautiful townland of Rinn Mhic Chiolla Rua, known as Ringmacilroy, so you can imagine how I felt when I watched its breathtaking scenery on Italian TV become the background to a horrific and well-documented massacre, on the same day that a close relative of Queen Elizabeth – Earl Mountbatten of Burma – was murdered across the border. Not only did I feel for those who had lost sons and husbands but for my parents and all the wonderful friends I had there who, like me, must have felt utterly ashamed, useless and traumatised. When it was announced – once again on Italian television – that a Customs man had been shot in his office, also in my home town, my worst fears were confirmed when my distraught mother broke the terrible news that it was our next-door neighbour's son, whom I had watched grow up from an old school pal into a gentle and lovely young man.

When Ivan Toombs first joined the civil service he accepted a post in London, where I was living at the time with three ex-college mates in a flat in Notting Hill Gate. The girls were great cooks, so that it became a home from home to all my pals, as news quickly circulated that the grub was good at 'Casa Marge'. Until he found somewhere permanent to live, Ivan stayed with our harem while, like so many other departed guests, still partaking of the excellent home-cooked Sunday lunches we dished out, even after he left us. I made the most terrible mistake by not writing to his family after his tragic death for the unforgivable reason that I didn't know what to say. Years later, after my return to Ulster, I was stopped in the street by a lady who introduced herself as Ivan's wife. She told me that their daughter was getting married and asked if I would sing at her wedding, even though she knew that I would command a high fee. When I told her that my singing would be on the house she said: 'I knew that you would do it for Ivan.' How right she was, since not only was I deeply honoured to be asked to participate in such a joyous event but it provided the opportunity to make amends for neglecting to acknowledge her husband's death.

On the day itself, while I was sitting in the choir stall waiting for the bride to arrive, I was approached by Ivan's son – with the same blond hair and fair complexion – who gave me a letter from his mother; inside, along with thirty pounds, was a beautiful, poignant letter, written that same morning, saying how proud Ivan would have been to have me sing at his daughter's wedding. It so happened that I already had my eye on a huge and outrageous clock with an alarm of burglar-like proportions which also cost thirty pounds. And so, soon after the wedding, I lost no time in buying it in memory of Ivan, who used to entertain his friends with stories about having to endure me practising my high notes into the early hours while they were trying to get some sleep next door. Although years have passed by, I still rely on that precious clock to get me up in time to catch ludicrously early flights to Milan and Rome.

When I told my mother that her kinsman, John McGuffin, had been interned in Belfast as a guest of Her Majesty's Government for his anarchistic views she said: 'Good for him. At last young people are speaking out in favour of what they think is right, instead of being told what to do according to their upbringing.' Her reaction didn't surprise me since I was blessed with an exceptionally liberally minded and totally unselfish mother who always put the needs of others before her own. When she died I received many letters about her love for everybody and everything, which wasn't entirely true, for when she disliked someone or something – always with good reason – she spared no punches, laced with her wicked sense of humour, which I inherited.

As she was born in the County Tyrone town of Dungannon, the eldest of four children, my mother's birth certificate was issued and signed by her own father, who was both local registrar of births, marriages and deaths, and clerk of the union and council. He was easily recognised by the long black cloak he wore as his trade mark, and became a force to be reckoned with when it came to protecting those in his care. As superintendent of the workhouse he fought hard with those in power for better living conditions for the underprivileged, living to fulfil his dream of transforming the workhouse into a splendid hospital, until government cuts eventually undid all his good work.

My mother's Christian name was Rachel which she hated so much that everyone called her Ray. In the early 1920s she trained as a teacher in Dublin before leaving Ireland to teach in Doncaster, in South Yorkshire. There she thrived in the county she took to her heart, translating the Yorkshire dialect for visiting southern English, simply because they spoke with similar expressions and Elizabethan vowel sounds to Ulster people. If she wasn't roaming the dales, in her free time she stayed and played golf in the grand spa hotels around Yorkshire and Llandudno in Wales. In retrospect, it must have been an extravagant lifestyle for a single woman of her generation – in comparison to the Methodist church, Sunday-school teaching way of life she would have led back home. But all that was to change when, on a visit home one Christmas, her brothers took her to a rugby dance, where she met and fell under the spell of the charming Samuel Wright, a man much sought after by ladies because of his gift of listening and looking at them with his 'spaniel eyes'. In the fullness of time, my mother forced herself to become immune to them, but I never could, worshipping the ground he walked on. Given that the Wright men were well known for fidelity and long courtships – anything up to fifteen years was the norm – she soon abandoned teaching to concentrate on getting her man to the church on time. Little did he know what the future held in store for him!

The Wrights were a completely different kettle of fish to the McGuffins: indeed it would be difficult to imagine any couple coming from two such incompatible backgrounds – in spite of the fact that my grandmother Wright just happened to be the aunt of my maternal one, making my parents second cousins! My musical friends who stayed with them when they were performing in Ireland used to remark on how similar in looks and mannerisms they were. At a loss for words – it happens – I would remark that, given enough time, people can even resemble their dogs! Eventually, my sister let the cat out of the bag when she revealed all, but, where I was concerned, they took their secret to their beautiful grave at the foot of the Mountains of Mourne, unaware that I knew.

My father's ancestors originally arrived in Ireland in the seventeenth century and settled in Gola in the county of Monaghan, which was then under British rule. I was under the impression that we came from Yorkshire until I was contacted by a certain Mr Wright, who, although no relation, informed me that a certain Captain James Wright of the Cambridge Light Infantry was the first Wright to arrive in Ireland and settle in Gola. There the breeding of future landowners and beasts of the highest quality all began. As the clan began to expand so did the amount of land they acquired, stretching across Co. Monaghan to as far north as Co. Fermanagh, all of which still remains in Ulster, even though today Co. Monaghan is situated in the Republic of Ireland, while the counties of Tyrone and Fermanagh are in the north. My grandfather was one of seven brothers who, in the wake of the potato famine, bought Elvey, which, after four generations, still remains in our family. I always maintain that if only that house could speak it would make a film worthy of an Oscar, for it was from there that my grandfather – a George Bernard Shaw lookalike – rode 'across the fields', like a knight in shining armour, to woo and marry the gregarious and exceptionally gifted Margaret Davidson. William and Margaret, by coincidence the same names as my maternal grandparents, certainly had a prolific marriage, as not only did the feisty Margaret become mum to two motherless children from her husband's first marriage but went on to produce ten of her own. Sadly, I never knew them, since they died long before I was even thought of, but I am constantly reminded of her by the gift of perfect pitch and rhythm which I inherited from her. Singing and playing the violin and piano were so inbred in the Elvey branch that, throughout my own professional career as a musician, I just took it for granted that everyone else was equally endowed. It wasn't until I was informed by a professor carrying out a survey at the Royal College of Music in London that perfect pitch was hereditary that I understood why my cousins could read hymns and music in the printed key without the aid of a piano. It just came naturally to them, and they weren't even professional musicians. Not all the tone-deaf Wrights married musical spouses and those who didn't were therefore considered musical pariahs by 'our lot', since the fruits of the land they inherited mainly produced clergymen and writers – not to mention a grass for the British government no less! One of my father's ancestors was a rector in the parish outside Newry in County Down where the Brontës' father, Patrick, had a school, before he and his Irish wife made literary history in Yorkshire. His Reverence even had the audacity to write a controversial book about the Brontës in 1888, the same year as my own father was born.

Dancing and teaching her children to sing was my grandmother's passion, instilling breathing and natural vocal technique into them from an early age. She was also the belle of the ball when local gentry invited her to perform the opening dance at their harvest balls, while she herself opened the Elvey barn for dancing on Saturday nights to neighbouring farmers and their families. After church on Sunday she would ride side-saddle over the country to distribute food to the poor, leaving her own twelve starving children waiting to be fed at home! But her kindness was not forgotten, even by the IRA, who promised that they would never touch Elvey, a Protestant stronghold, perched right on the border, as long as the Wright family lived there. They kept their word.

My aunt said that Elvey always kept a gentleman. Thus spoke the expert since she cooked, cleaned and looked after the remaining flock, as soon as my uncle Willie brought her home as a bride. She was of course referring to my father and my cousin Wallace – who succeeded him in the role. Not only did they both dress to kill but were the star attraction as eligible bachelors. Wallace was the youngest of 'the five boys' on the farm, and, while my sister and I followed him around with adoring eyes, my mother considered him to be a cross between an Adonis and a Lawrence Olivier lookalike. But there was one article of clothing that Wallace was particularly fond of: a Fair Isle pullover. When my father and I arrived at the house on the day of his brother's wedding we were met with a scene of sheer pandemonium, caused by best man Wallace's refusal to wear a waistcoat instead of his beloved pullover. When his two brothers saw me they dragged me into the sitting room where Wallace was being held prisoner. There, Operation Pullover began: as they held him down on the floor, I pulled it off while, to screams of protest, I managed to replace the Fair Isle with his smart suit's matching waistcoat.

But while Wallace was not afraid to dirty his hands and do his bit around the farm, his Uncle Sam was. When my father was given the job of feeding the horses, along with his pet donkey and zebra pony, he was relieved of the task after his own favourites showed symptoms of an oats overdose; in fact he was to perfect this trick of pretending to be useless to great effect throughout his entire life. But my fondest 'Daddy story' is the one about him deciding to take time off at home to perfect his art and devote more time to practising the violin. As the 'sabbatical' visit became more prolonged my grandfather came up with the perfect plan to restore peace at Elvey and send the prodigal son packing. And so, one morning the old man harnessed his horse to a trap and conducted him to the nearest town. There he pulled up at the local hardware shop where the unsuspecting Sam was presented with a shovel and spade. By nightfall he was gone!

Although we all love to sing in our family – never an occasion passes by without a sing-song which I loathe so much that I am ordered to close my ears and play the piano – it is the violin which is in our blood. Before Hillsborough Castle became the official residence of the UK government Secretary of State to Northern Ireland, it was privately owned by the Hill family who, for some reason or other, were auctioning some enticing and valuable items, among which was a beautiful violin which my father bought for six pennies. Without questioning its value he made the huge mistake of leaving it behind at Elvey, where it remained in the hands of future generations. No longer living at home, and without his beloved violin, he had to buy another one, which I also used and took to London in its much-admired case of pigskin leather with S.D.W. – his initials – embossed in gold. Back at the home farm the grand one hung on the back of the parlour door waiting for my uncle Willie, and his namesake son, to play after a hard day on the farm. But it was Willie junior who had the talent and, in my eyes, musical genius. When we visited, my father and he would spend hours together discussing their own version of how a violin and piano should be played. Even when my father was on his deathbed Willie was still talking to him about HOW to get the best out of an instrument. Little did I know that I too would carry on the family tradition of pacing and breathing and use it to help others in my book *The Wright Way to Breathe*. After Willie junior's death, his daughter decided to have the Hillsborough violin valued. You can imagine the shock she got when she found out that the 'cheap' violin bought for six pennies by her great-uncle Sam was a precious and rare Cremona. While I was over the moon to be asked to play it for the first time at my cousin Willie and his long-suffering wife Annie's golden wedding party, the main problem was how to get it out of Elvey, since other than sleeping with it, Willie never let it out of his sight! The sheer joy on his face said it all when I appeared, his favourite uncle's own daughter, playing the cherished heirloom. Later he couldn't resist winding me up by remarking that, apart from my being a little rusty, my bowing arm was a bit stiff!

Such was my dream to play in a big symphony orchestra that I fervently practised to achieve it when I chose the violin as my second subject at the Royal College of Music. I was so keen to play well that my singing teacher, who had no time for my gin-drinking violin professor who sat in a chair and did nothing, that he most generously tried to pull strings so that I could study with the great Brazilian violinist Antonio Brosa. Unfortunately we were thwarted when my useless professor accused us of conspiracy and undermining him, while – at the same time – reminding me that I was on an Associated Board Scholarship for singing, and not violin. Nevertheless, I achieved my graduate teaching diploma in violin, only because there was no singing teacher on Saturday mornings in the junior department of the college, a post which was joyously filled by yours truly once I graduated!! Throughout my singing career, which others have quite rightly envied, and still do, I have been plagued by those who cannot understand why I don't sing for pleasure, but will play a keyboard or organ at the drop of a hat. In retrospect, I didn't choose singing as my career: it was chosen for me by people in the business who considered I had a better chance of making a success with my vocal ability than with the instruments I love. Perhaps that is why people are shocked when I tell them that singing was only my job, and that I love my one-woman show, which transports me back to my uninhibited musical childhood, when I could sing to my own piano accompaniment before my feet could reach the pedals.

In the twilight of my trials and tribulations, it is wonderful to reflect that my parents never influenced me in my decisions. My mother's opinion was that children should leave the nest around 18 years of age and be welcomed home at any time with open arms. This is exactly what happened when my sister and I were offered opportunities in London that we couldn't refuse. Our careers and lives 'across the water' transported our parents into a world so outside their – then – narrow confines that when things got tough I journeyed on, so as not to disappoint them. When I eventually confessed to my mother that I felt uncomfortable and a misfit in the difficult, back-biting world of professional singing she said – in her typical blunt Ulster style: 'You chose it, we didn't. You made your own bed, so you must lie on it.' I lay on it!!

Surely a family can suffer no greater loss than that of a child. My two sisters, Helen and Joan, were born just over two years apart and were inseparable playmates. Six years before I was born, Joan, who was only 2½ years old, caught whooping cough, which rapidly developed into double pneumonia. Within a week she was gone. Such was the impact of her death on Helen and our parents that her name was even too painful to mention, while I was left in limbo with a photo album of a happy family of four, with Joan perched on my mother's knee and Helen on my father's. How they recovered I shall never know – my sister never did. In retrospect I wonder if it explained the close bond between my father and his cousin, the Reverend Jackson Wright, of whom I have wonderful childhood memories. Although Jackson was full of fun and great with children, he had served time in the forces and must have dealt with unimaginable suffering when he was chaplain to the Ulster Division at the Battle of the Somme. Later this exceptional human being left the army and took up a post as rector in a small town in Northern Ireland, where he became great friends with the local resident magistrate. Unfortunately Jackson forgot, like the rest of our family, that there were other people on the road who also drove and – in this case – walked, until one day he knocked down an on-duty policeman who wasted no time in capitalising on such a conquest. In a scene reminiscent of *The Irish RM* and *The Quiet Man*, the rector was summoned and brought to account before his friend in a courtroom filled to capacity with his own parishioners and those from other religious denominations. He was lucky to get off with a fine and a severe warning.

At the time of Joan's death my parents were living in the same Belfast neighbourhood as my mother's cousin, the MP Sam McGuffin, to whom she was very close. When Northern Ireland was entirely ruled from Westminster Uncle Sam represented the Shankill area of Belfast as a Labour MP and become known as 'a man of the people', completely without airs and graces. During the partition of Ulster he, along with Craigavon – the first leader in the new parliament – opposed the idea of a separate ruling body being set up at Stormont; when they were overruled Uncle Sam continued to represent his constituents as their Labour Unionist MP, eventually being appointed Speaker. The rest is history!

My sister spent a lot of time with Uncle Sam and his wife during that tragic time in my parents' lives, during which he introduced her to stocks and shares at an early age; no wonder she married an accountant and produced two sons and a grandson who have followed suit. He also must have passed on the McGuffin tradition of standing up for the rights of others to his nephew John, who became famous – or dare I say infamous – as a criminal lawyer and resistance writer, circling the world to defend those suffering from maltreatment. When I myself became a victim of gruesome injustice I called upon those same genes to give me the strength to voice my opinion on behalf of, and write about, the stigma and degradation inflicted on those who are too afraid to speak out and think for themselves. If I hadn't been blessed with that inherited gift I wouldn't be alive today to share my extraordinary story with you.

# Act I

# Scene 1

## *Ritorno in Patria* (Back Home)

When I lived in Italy I was unable to understand why bookcases in my Italian friends' homes contained so many volumes of works by James Joyce. As an Irishwoman I had to shamefully admit that the writings of my nation's national treasure were too pedantic for my taste. But it was when I was invited to sing the role of the mother in *Ulysses*, written by my guru, the great Italian composer Luigi Dallapiccola, that I became immersed in the story of this great King of Ithaca who began his long journey back to his homeland from the Trojan wars. Dallapiccola's approach to this character was based on the Ulysses in Homer's *Odyssey*, and not that written by Joyce, but when I happened to mention to him that the role of the mother brought out a hitherto unknown Irish streak in me, he revealed that since Ulysses had no mother in Homer's *Odyssey* he drew on Joyce's *Ulysses* and so when it was performed in Paris, it was sung by an authentic Irishwoman – yours truly! Such was the impact made on me by performing this wonderfully powerful role in Italian that I understood why Joyce was so revered in Italy, after I read his powerful writing translated into that most beautiful of all languages. And so, when politics raised its ugly head and my career began to go pear-shaped, I set forth on my own odyssey from the wars of unions and musical intrigue back to my homeland via London, Norwich and Ryanair.

Even today those involved in the politics that govern the Italian music industry cannot understand how I can be without rancour, after

I was reported to the unions by two soprano colleagues who accused me – a foreigner and intruder – of depriving them of the bread and butter which, in their eyes, should have been on their tables and not mine. I had already been warned that they were out for my blood by other kind colleagues who were themselves scared of these two women, who had such powerful connections that they remained a threat to anyone who stood in their way – lasting long after their singing days were over and they were appointed professors in distinguished music conservatoires. If their students left them they would make sure that they would live to regret it, leaving me with no other option but to face the fact that if they could do it to their own I didn't stand a chance.

Up until the 1970s I was having a blissful time as a solo concert singer, performing both classical and contemporary music with first-class professionals, mainly in Italy and Vienna, where I formed a lieder duo with Rainer Keuschnig, who at that time was resident pianist with the Vienna Philharmonic. Among the fantastic ensembles I had the joy of working with was the Ensemble Kontrapunckte, made up of Vienna's finest orchestral musicians and conducted by Rainer's brother Peter. Not only did we make exciting music together but had great fun 'on location' finding the best places to eat and drink wine, of which we consumed a lot. I had never ever considered a career as an opera singer because, apart from it not being in my blood, I was a musician who sang and played the classics. A true opera singer must yearn to sing and transform themselves into heroes and heroines far removed from reality, whereas I like to dress in the clothes I choose and inhabit my own individual and down-to-earth world. The only occasions when I performed as an opera singer were in concert form and not in a live staged production; so when I was asked to sing the role of yet another mother in Dallapiccola's *The Prisoner,* I had – purely through lack of experience – enormous difficulty adjusting to working with and keeping up with real first-class opera singers, who, as it turned out, could not have been more helpful and understanding. Indeed, throughout my short-lived venture into the world of opera, I was to meet colleagues who not only worked as a team but had the utmost respect for one another; as a result, I became close friends with many who – considered to be difficult-to-work-with prima donnas by managements and agents on whom we depended for our livelihood – turned out to be pussies underneath the facade which is needed to protect us from scandal and gossip-mongers.

Life on the international singing circuit can be a lonely one, especially if you are a solo concert performer; but the great plus to the individual traveller is that one is usually away in a strange country for no longer than a week at a time and if a difficult conductor makes one's life a misery, then it is short lived and can be endured. I am delighted to tell you that there are only a few to be found in my black book of horrors. Opera, on the other hand, can take a singer away from home for anything up to six weeks – including rehearsals and performances – so that while getting on with your mates for a long sojourn is a must, a great sense of camaraderie can be an uplifting and beautiful experience. I was lucky to get so much work because I was a modern-music specialist, the requirements for which were: an ability to pitch notes at random and to change rhythm every other bar, cast-iron vocal chords, nerves of steel and an ability to memorise music bereft of tunes. In Italy, because singers who had these qualifications were in short supply at that time – now, with wonderful teachers and advanced techniques, there is an abundance – the services of the same team of specialists were called on to cope with the demands of 'academic' composers, like Karl Heinz Stockhausen, and men of great learning. Not only did we have to get on together as a squad, but we did with considerable ease. It may surprise you to know that throughout my time working in Italian concert halls and opera houses I never heard an Italian musician speak badly about another – such was the respect that one artiste had for another.

My male operatic colleagues particularly suffered from bouts of homesickness and missed their wives and families more than the ladies missed their loved ones; but then we were prima donnas who loved to shop and look the part in mink coats and the latest Italian fashion, especially when we all – male and female – had the finest boutiques of Venice at our disposal. Even now, in my twilight years, to reminisce about performing at Teatro La Fenice, Venice's famous opera house, is surreal. The Venetians are fun people with a very dry sense of humour which I just love. We have always enjoyed a special chemistry and bond between us which continues to this day, as you will discover when I am reborn in Act 2! Nevertheless, being away from home, paying one's hotel and travel expenses, not to mention eating in good restaurants – in order to keep up appearances – can be costly. It was in Venice that we were left in a state of financial distress when a powerful earthquake destroyed nearby Friuli before reaching Venice with an eight-grade impact. I had just finished my evening meal in a restaurant off St Mark's Square when the tables turned upside down, as the sand and water from the lagoon surged underneath the floor and alleys outside the building. Against the forces of nature one has little chance, so I took to my heels and made for the open space of St Mark's Square only to discover that my tenor colleague, an amateur geologist and voice of doom in the prediction of earthquakes, had already found space on steps commanding a view of the steeple beside the famous basilica. It wasn't until he asked if I could swim that I realised that we were on a lagoon!!! The entire scene eclipsed any of the ones we were currently rehearsing when he turned to me and said: 'Don't be afraid, Wright; I am a champion swimmer and will keep you afloat.' Back on dry land, the theatre had to be declared safe before we could continue to rehearse and perform. Under Italian *Forza Maggiore* – major forces in English – one cannot claim damages or insurance if they are caused by an outbreak of war or an earthquake, since the latter is considered to be an act of God. This would have meant that not only would we not have been paid but we would have been left to pay our own hotel bills and expenses from our bank accounts, minus the good fees on which we depended. Fortunately the theatre was declared safe and we were allowed to perform. Most of the audience aimed for the seats nearer the doors, since it was rather difficult to distinguish between the slight remaining earth tremors circling the city and the wash from the boats in the canal.

When I lived in Milan while working in Turin, just over an hour away by train, I was able to get home after a Sunday matinee performance at the impressive Teatro Regio, since Monday is a day of rest in theatres. My colleague, the late and wonderful soprano Emilia Ravaglia, who lived further away, had to remain in her hotel room, which she transformed into a home from home. We used to describe her arrival as 'Emilia's *trasloco*', because she seemed to bring her entire household commodities along with her. Although the hotel had a restaurant, delicious, mouth-watering smells drifted down the corridor from her room, including roasted red peppers, which I adored. Emilia was also a great knitter, as she believed it was good therapy to help her cope with the difficult music we had to deliver. I teased her unmercifully after a sweater she was knitting turned into a dress. She had the last laugh when, inspired by her enthusiasm and encouragement, I knitted a scarf, which must be the longest on record. I still wear it to shield my vocal chords from wintry winds. Sadly, my roller coaster musical ride was to come to an abrupt end after I was asked to sing the role of Michelangelo's spiritual mistress, Vittoria Colonna, at the world famous La Scala, Milan, in preference to the two Italian sopranos who had been 'deposed'. I began to become suspicious after I was replaced by one of the 'two ugly sisters' at two upcoming concerts on the grounds that the Questura – the Italian police headquarters – had refused permission for me to sing. Smelling a rat, I immediately got in touch with a friend who was first secretary at the Irish embassy in Rome. She gave me the vital information I needed as a member of the European community to take to the police, who could not have been more welcoming and charming. They were in total agreement with the Irish embassy as I declared in loud tones that I was legally entitled to sing whatever and wherever I liked in Italy because, under European law, a *permesso di sogiorno* (a permission to stay) was abolished for British and Irish citizens. Since the whole scenario turned out to be an entire fabrication anyway, my friends and I knew that the writing was on the wall: and so, after long hours of deliberation and soul searching we decided that it would be more practical for me to return to London where, in my case, such problems would not exist, apart from the fact that I would be entitled to financial assistance from the state, as well as an assured pension. While we agonised over being parted, my Italian team of supporters and I consoled ourselves by my commuting to Italy as a visiting artiste. But it didn't quite turn out that way once London opened up a new world to me as a writer and campaigner for human rights, leaving the stresses of singing to simmer on the back burner.

Walking out of Hatchards – the royal booksellers in London's Piccadilly – with a surprise order for twelve copies of my first 'baby', *How To Be A Bad Singer!*, was the greatest thrill of my life, after a friend dared me to go inside and 'flog' it. Teaching in Italy had given me such pleasure and feedback that I wanted to share it with those who might not have been so lucky, since good students are a rare find. But then not all teachers are as generous as the late and great American/Armenian singer Cathy Berberian, who, having heard one of my talented students perform, directed pop stars, actors and you name them, in my direction. All of them were hungry to learn and stretched my teaching techniques to the limit, not to mention leaving me a nervous and exhausted wreck after their departure. But it was fun and we all loved each other and the uninhibited exchange of banter; in fact it was after I confided in Cathy that there were complaints from other teachers about the laughter coming from my room at the posh academy where I taught that she filled my studio at home with even more.

I had intended my rather tattered, home-made edition of *How To Be A Bad Singer!* to be used in workshops, never imagining that it would go on public display. I had a hard job convincing my bank manager to lend me £1,000 for further production until he relented, on condition that the loan would be paid back within a month – he meant it. And so, I had no other option but to add yet another string to my bow: my own sales representative. I was having a ball, liberated from the restrictions of the classical music world, wearing casual clothes instead of 'putting on my silver shoes' at eight o'clock, as described by a colleague. It never occurred to us that lots of women would have given their eye teeth to dress up in our 'uniform'. Eventually *HTBABS!* was taken over by a real publisher and launched in 1989. It is still in print today, in 2013, and now has a pal, *The Wright Way To Breathe*.

When I launched it in Northern Ireland, the Troubles had still not been resolved. The resilience of such wonderful people to turn out to support and encourage me was so heart-rending that I felt it my duty to give back something to those whose own teaching skills had given me opportunities of which musicians could only dream. I had been away from my roots for so long that I was beginning to have an identity crisis, and so I packed my bags and set off across the Irish Sea, from where my musical odyssey began, to bring musical peace to Ulster. Once again, it didn't quite turn out that way.

The magical town land of Ringmacilroy, with the mountains sweeping down to the sea, is the ideal place for writers and artistes to live, which one can so selfishly take for granted until visiting friends and tourists remind me of how privileged I am to be inspired by such beauty, which they themselves would have given their eye teeth to have. But, once the honeymoon was over, it didn't take me long to discover that life as a writer and teacher in Ireland was a very different ball game from the cushy one I had as a singer; all I had to do was perform in different countries and leave the job, before returning to base to prepare for the next one without being interrupted by self-promotion or spoken interviews. I was to discover that life had moved on from those good old days when one was taken on merit and face value, to the age of celebrity and being packaged into a commodity. Not only did one have to sell one's own product, but to dress and make up for public display which, in my case, was a public intrusion into my privacy. What mainly irritated veterans and real opera singers was the presentation of colleagues who had never taken part in a real full-length operatic production referred to as opera divas, while they themselves had spent years perfecting roles and establishing a cast-iron technique to preserve their voices for such demanding work. Relieved of all this paraphernalia, I was forced to remove the mask behind which I had been hiding for so long to reveal my real identity – which I had reserved only for those that I love and trust – after *How To Be A Bad Singer!* introduced me into the world of showbiz and a new set of friends, completely divorced from the elite world of music which I had inhabited.

It all began when Sean Rafferty – the presenter of BBC Radio 3's *In Tune* programme – heard that I had returned to Ulster and invited me to talk about *HTBABS!* on his morning chat show on BBC Radio Ulster. So many years had passed since Sean had interviewed me for a programme about the Irish in Rome that both our respective heads of hair had turned white, yet the same chemistry and humour between us was still alive. One programme about HRT nearly caused a car pile-up on the M1.

My suspicions were first aroused when Sean's office rang to invite me to a performance of *Women On The Verge Of HRT* by Marie Jones, the brilliant Ulster playwright, which I was to discuss on his programme the following morning. It didn't take long to discover the reason for my involvement in Sean's popular show after a rather nervous lady took her seat beside me in the box overlooking the stage in Belfast's Grand Opera House. As we chatted over a glass of wine and goodies provided by the BBC she told me that she was also an invited guest but was so terrified and overawed by the magnitude of the occasion that she didn't know if her nerves would survive the ordeal of a live broadcast the following morning. Over more generous BBC hospitality in the interval I tried to comfort her by telling her that from personal experience I could assure her Sean was such a brilliant and compassionate interviewer that she would forget she was even on air.

Next morning, on my way into the hospitality room, I happened to tell the chatty receptionist, whom I already knew quite well, about my own personal experiences with HRT, never imagining that I was providing 'food for the fodder'. What I didn't know was that Marie Jones herself would be taking part in the programme. As an ardent fan I was thrilled to meet her and had just begun chatting to her about my forthcoming one-woman show at the Lyric Theatre when we were interrupted by the arrival of the lady from the previous evening who, overnight, had not only found her voice but brought all the poems she had written to show to Marie. By the time we were ushered into the studio we were so well warmed up that all Sean had to do was to join in! Once on air our mystery guest grasped the opportunity to inform the province that not only was she a member of the Belfast Abused Women's Organisation but was certainly not in need of HRT because she had just had a hysterectomy! Marie and I didn't get a word in edgeways until Sean turned to me and asked me about my opinion on HRT. By the time the programme had ended the entire province knew that my GP had taken me off the replacement drug because he thought I was slightly OTT, to which Sean added, 'You were just being your normal self, Marjorie.'

During those fun times at the BBC I met the most wonderful talent and people originating from there with charming, down-to-earth personalities. It was during a programme about teaching methods, which was being specially made in Belfast for BBC Radio Scotland, that I first met the classical guitarist Martin McAllister, with whom I formed an instant rapport – once I told him that I was researching the sequel to *HTBABS!* to include breathing for instrumentalists. Martin comes from South Armagh which, at that time, was more associated with cross-border terrorist activities and atrocities than the people who live there. I have always had a place in my heart for this part of the world as I used to accompany my mother and her teacher friends on smuggling trips to Dundalk, where they would cross the border in old clothes which they threw into a field before returning, bold as brass, before the Customs officers clad in the latest fashion that the town had to offer. To be given the opportunity to coach these hungry-to-learn young people was a rare privilege, as it brought back wonderful memories of similar chemistry shared with my eclectic group of students in Milan. Coming from a part of the world where Irish culture is embraced to its full potential – from Gaelic football to ceilidh bands and Irish dancing – Martin's students were only too delighted to incorporate my breathing tips into their art, while I was only too honoured to contribute.

There is always a moment in a teacher's life when they feel that it has all been worthwhile. It happened to me when a tenor suffering from clinical depression sought my help as a last resort; he was also a lucky to have a friend who was willing to listen and point him in my direction. John certainly didn't resemble what I had imagined him to be; instead of a depressed and introverted person, I was confronted by a tall and deeply tanned man. When I inquired if he had got it on holiday he explained that his healthy appearance was due to his employment by the local council as a helper to his loyal friend – who just happened to be their head gardener – in the hope that work and fresh air would be preferable to sitting at home under sedation. He also explained that he was a classically trained singer, but found great difficulty in recapturing his love of singing. You can imagine the jubilation in my studio when I discovered that a deep, rich sound emerged from John's vocal chords once I had showed him how to use certain muscles and breathe through the whole body, instead of confining it to the chest region. For years I had sung as a soprano after my deep contralto voice was 'misdiagnosed'; once it returned to its natural habitat, I was released from all the pent-up emotion and vocal tension and took on a new lease of life. In John's case it only took an hour before he was set free to enjoy the same experience – like an animal being released from a cage. As he drove off I shouted, 'Throw away the pills!' He did.

When I lived in Milan a priest came to bless my apartment at Easter and Christmas, which, although I am a Christian, made me feel so ashamed as I hadn't been to church for such a long time. During one of this lovely man's holy week visits I suddenly felt the urge to go to church. When I confessed that I was an Ulster Protestant he was much amused, reassuring me that I had a direct line to God and was not to feel guilty about 'cutting out the middle man'. It was then I realised how much I missed the wonderful repertoire of English church music in which one could indulge. Before moving to Italy I had been a member of the world-famous group the Ambrosian Singers, directed by the late John McCarthy. When we weren't recording or performing we provided the music for Sunday services, weddings and memorials – usually in groups of four – around London's beautiful churches. For me it was a labour of love for which I was being paid. Although we weren't members of the regular Sunday choir at All Souls, Langham Place, I have vivid memories of the music and people at whose weddings and memorials we sang, as it just happened to be next door to Broadcasting House. Since we were hardened professionals we usually turned up on time, did the job and went home without batting an eyelid, unless the 'protagonist' was someone special. On one occasion I felt privileged and proud when I realised that the distinguished man being remembered at All Souls was the Ulster poet and playwright Louis MacNeice who had been with the BBC for some years. Singing 'Beatus Vir' by the composer Bencini was particularly emotional and beautiful, not to mention the crowning moment when MacNeice's great friend, the poet W. H. Auden, gave the address, standing in front of my pew. Years later I watched BBC Northern Ireland's excellent documentary on the poet. Unaware that his father had been the Bishop of Connor, I was even more interested when the camera brought the viewer to beautiful Carrickfergus on the shores of Belfast Lough, where MacNeice's father had been rector of St Nicholas's Church and where he had spent his early childhood before the tragic loss of his mother. I was even more surprised when a former rector's wife, who just happened to be married to my father's cousin, appeared in the garden of St Nicholas's rectory to inform us that it had been influential in inspiring him to write his poetry, reminding one of the loss C. S. Lewis suffered when his mother died in Belfast during his childhood, inspiring him in later life to write the 'Chronicles of Narnia'. I had no idea that Canon Robert Wright, my father's cousin, had been a successor to MacNeice's father at St Nicholas's Church, let alone a lecturer and expert on his work; in turn, he was equally surprised when I told him that I had sung at his memorial service in the presence of Auden, a copy of whose address on that occasion Robert happened to have in his personal possession. A small world indeed.

Not long after my return to Ringmacilroy in the mid-1990s, a stroke of good fortune presented itself when a real-life 'middle man of the cloth' showed up at my front door, with whom I was to form an enduring friendship until his premature death. Since the local Anglican church is my neighbour I couldn't avoid saying hello to the recently appointed young rector, Julian McCready. In true Irish tradition he knew who I was, and I knew that he was the son of the famous Irish theatre director and writer Sam McCready who, apart from resembling the Irish poet Yeats, is a world expert on the great man's work. I had sung as a young girl in a choir directed by the incumbent church organist – an F.R.C.O – who just happened to have been offered a superior post immediately before the harvest thanksgiving 'over the wall', leaving poor Julian in desperate need of musical help. And so, when he turned up on my doorstep at his wit's end, I had no other option but to oblige a neighbour in distress. I stayed for two years.

Well aware of the organ's reputation for stiffness and generally giving those who had the courage to play it a hard time, my first task was to make friends by calling it Gertie. Before she was modernised Gertie had been 'driven' by sea water so it was imperative that the swimming baths were not emptied at the same time that services took place. But nobody told me about the blast of air that circled round the feet of the organist, prompting kind parishioners to bring me scarves and woollen hats to protect me from the draught. As my confidence grew, Gertie began to respond, once Julian pulled out stops which produced a decent sound and which I didn't dare disturb on the two-manual instrument. But once I audaciously applied the pedals to my self-taught technique, I was off. I also sang lustily with the choir who, with time, learnt to punctuate and sing the psalms like a dream.

We were indeed a happy lot, introducing brides and bridegrooms to wonderfully rousing hymns and music, stretching from their own choice to Mozart, Cesar Franck's 'Panis Angelicus' and Walton's 'Crown Imperial'. Since we aimed to please, we didn't forget to allow the less fortunate members of the congregation to choose funeral music for their loved ones. But there was one request for which the printed music was only found on our way to the service – since burial in Ireland usually takes place two days after demise – which I included in the music to which the deceased was carried out of the church. Some months later when his widow accused me of not respecting her wishes, I was able to tell her that I had played it as 'variations on a theme' on the music that her beloved husband would have wanted.

On a fun occasion as I arrived to play for a wedding at a beautiful 13th-century country church looking out over the Mountains of Mourne, I imagined I was witnessing a scene straight out of the TV series *The Vicar of Dibley* after a neighbouring farmer had forgotten to properly close the gate to the field from which his flock of cattle were making their way to the wedding across the road. As the frightened bridesmaids emerged from the car Julian, dressed in his cassock, was chasing the animals away from the church door and adjoining cemetery, while I marshalled the assembling guests and bridal party back to their cars, just as the farmer arrived to claim his herd. By the time the bride arrived everything had been brought under control and the show carried on. Sadly, all good things must come to an end, and after Julian and his wife Florence left Ireland to reside in England, it was also time for me to focus on my new career as a writer and finding a publisher for *The Rise and Fall of a La Scala Diva.*

As a contemporary music specialist I was enormously privileged to work with living composers and spent many treasured hours in their company learning about the written texts of great writers and poets who inspired their compositions. When I was rehearsing 'Commiato' – a work for soprano soloist and chamber ensemble – in Florence I asked the composer, Luigi Dallapiccola, to record Bruno Latini's beautiful prayer 'O Fratel Nostro' to which he had set his gloriously difficult music. I still treasure that wonderful Italian text, which is the only known recording of the maestro's voice as he disliked being interviewed. When I began to write myself I felt liberated from attempting, as a singer, to interpret the thoughts of others in the hope that I was conveying the true meaning and conception of what I was singing about. And so, instead of boring my friends with my endless opinions and stories on subjects in which they were not interested, I decided to write them down and target them at those who were.

'A Broth of a Girl' was a short story about the secret life I led outside the world of music, while 'The Warrenpoint Warbler' was much grander and directed to a more elitist form of reader whom I imagined would have been shocked by the 'other me'. When I confided in one or two friends belonging to the Italian musical hierarchy that I wasn't quite the serious singer they had previously employed they were tickled pink and admitted that they had already guessed and couldn't wait to read my books. I had already started a novel, aided and abetted by my girlfriends, called 'Love On A High Note', but that came to an abrupt halt when, having just completed a chapter in which the conductor fainted while conducting an opera, fiction tragically turned into reality after I switched on the radio the following morning to hear the devastating news that my friend the Venetian conductor Giuseppe Sinopoli had collapsed and died the previous evening while conducting *Aida* in Berlin. I had met Giuseppe many years before he became world famous at the Biennale in Venice when he had already qualified as a medical doctor before becoming a composer. He was a man of enormous charm and charisma, completely without airs and graces. When my friends at the Autumn Festival on Lake Como asked me to perform one of Giuseppe's compositions I had to refuse the engagement because the tessitura was outside my range. Some time later, when I accidently bumped into him in Venice, it gave me the opportunity to personally explain the reason for my refusal; you can imagine my relief when he admitted that he too was relieved when he heard that I had turned him down, as when he wrote the piece he had a much lighter soprano voice in mind than my heavyweight one. Venice came to a halt when it honoured Giuseppe with a funeral procession down the Grand Canal, the like of which has not been seen since that of Stravinsky, who is also buried there.

My writing progressed alongside the growth of technology, beginning on a simple typewriter, then an electric one, before I succumbed to a computer, which terrified the wits out of me. Both of my autobiographical stories were merged into one as 'The Disappearing Diva', a title I invented to catch the eye of the reader and not because I considered myself to be one. After a number of rejections from reputable publishers telling me that although they liked my book it wasn't suitable for their list, I was overjoyed when I got a letter from Sandy Leung, the then managing director of Janus Publishing, with the news I had been waiting for: he would be honoured to publish 'The Disappearing Diva'.

Although their office was in London, I had to go to their printing premises in Colchester to complete formalities and meet Janus's friendly staff, with whom I had already made contact by phone and email. And so, with mounting excitement and anticipation, I booked a flight from Belfast to Stanstead Airport, en route to the ancient Roman town for the meeting which was to change my life for ever.

My first impression of Sandy Leung, who was of Chinese origin, was of a mature Lang Lang – his compatriot and world-acclaimed pianist. They certainly shared the same charisma and a dramatic impact on those who met them. I nearly exploded when he suggested changing 'The Disappearing Diva' for another title: 'I want to explain why I disappeared!'

'But you haven't,' he said. 'You are sitting before me, as large as life. That title will never sell, so you must think of another one and let me know.'

Then, just as I was about to leave, Sandy came up with *The Rise And Fall of a Scala Diva* which couldn't have been more appropriate, as I did rise and fall. It was to be the only time I would meet Sandy for, not long after our meeting, he handed over the reins to his daughter, Jeannie. Sadly, much to everyone's great sorrow, he passed away prematurely a few months after the Italian translation of the eye-catching title he chose was awarded the Leone d'Argento life achievement award in Venice.

# Scene 2
# Magical Moments

As I became accustomed to a lifestyle far removed from the world I had inhabited as a singer, a piece of me still yearned for the unexpected, real-life dramas it produced, so far removed from normality. My colleagues had either retired from performing in public and taught – since the amount of performing one can deliver takes its toll over the years – or preferred to just live with their memories. Not only were they incredibly generous and bemused when I put mine into words but joined into my new world with the same gusto and camaraderie we had all once shared. You can imagine how overwhelmed I was when none other than the great German composer Karl Heinz Stockhausen became a 'fan', even though I had never performed his music! We became 'pen pals' when I asked his permission to write in *The Rise and Fall of a La Scala Diva* about my visit to his home in Cologne, never imagining for one moment that he would remember me. But he did.

At that time he was looking for someone to replace a soprano on a tour of Germany. Since it was written for a black singer we agreed that if he couldn't find one he would rewrite some of the work to accommodate me – a white singer. It wasn't long before he discovered my dear friend, the black American Annette Meriweather, who became indispensable to him; in fact it was she who encouraged me to get in touch with the great maestro, as, knowing we were friends, he had already told her about my visit to his beautiful home in the woods. As well as encouraging me to write and give hope to musicians who had fallen on hard times, he gave his personal blessing for Janus Publishing to use the photo of him on the back cover of my autobiography. I couldn't help but notice Stockhausen's resemblance to the great English composer John Tavener, with similar long blond hair and impressive build, except that Tavener was exceptionally tall.

Pensioners in Ireland are able to travel free by public transport throughout the entire country, enabling one to meet an eclectic mix of retired people enjoying the sights and opportunities so generously offered. But while others were glad to be relieved of the stresses of work I was at last given the opportunity to realise my dream of becoming a vocal doctor, repairing voices and throats which had been damaged through either wrong diagnosis or being starved of oxygen. Soon so many people, from teachers to metal rock singers, were contacting my 'surgery' that my first baby, *How To Be A Bad Singer!*, was well on the way to having a sibling. Through my Saturday morning get-togethers in my large sitting room I was also able to develop my love of cooking and entertaining when we would retire to the kitchen where young singers, ranging from classical and heavy metal enthusiasts to traditional, would discuss the same basic technique of finding their own voices over a pizza or a favourite dish.

Out of this gathering emerged one of the most experimental and fulfilling achievements of my life as a musician when one of this lovely group, who had absorbed everything I had to dish out (including the food) arrived out of the blue one day to beg me to take her friend and classmate for singing lessons, except that it was no ordinary request. Danielle and Aideen were both preparing for their GCSE, due to take place in the spring/summer of the following year, leaving me little time to prepare her for the Grade 5 Associated Board practical necessary to qualify for the school exam. When I was informed that Aideen had never had a singing lesson in her life, I firmly refused to take her on as a potential student: but Danielle wouldn't take no for an answer and had already arranged for Aideen and her mother to meet her at my house within the hour. When Aideen's mother told me that her daughter had Crohn's disease, a debilitating bowel illness, I was firmly convinced that it would be mission impossible. Yet I was so moved by

Danielle' gesture on behalf of her friend that I eventually gave in on condition that I would not be held responsible if she failed. Even the secretary at the Associated Board's office in London thought it rather a challenge to jump four grades and attempt the fifth in a few months' time without my ever having taught her, but she duly sent the entry form and asked me to let them know the result! And so, Aideen and I began our adventure. Not only did she turn out to be the ideal student, but she looked the part. Before her illness she had studied ballet and had a great sense of rhythm, which enabled her to move and get her voice into the muscles using the tape I made of the songs we had chosen. Thomas Arne's 'Where The Bee Sucks' suited her dainty style down to the ground, making her the ideal Associated Board candidate, whereas Vaughan Williams' 'Linden Lea' was not quite Danielle's cup of tea; yet her unaccompanied singing of the haunting Irish folk song 'She Moved Through the Fair' was something else, as she was really a true traditional Irish singer. After a lot of hard work Danielle, Aideen and I set off for the exam, which was held at my old school. When we were ushered into the examination room, which just happened to be the former kitchen where my domestic science teacher hated me so much that I had to be removed from her class, my heart sank in case her ghost might haunt us; but the kitchen must have been exorcised during the building's redevelopment for all went according to plan, as well as my decision to accompany them at the piano myself. When the results came out Aideen got more marks than Danielle, so that I had a difficult job explaining to Danielle's parents why Aideen had accomplished so much in a few months, while their daughter had taken a few years. Nevertheless, we were all overjoyed that such a lovely talented girl, who a year before had been unable to walk, got her high grades in both exams, despite long absences from school.

When I discovered that the South African-born actress Janet Suzman was to give a workshop to drama students at the Belfast Festival at Queen's University, I simply had to go to absorb everything this great actress had to deliver. Not only was she the niece of the incredible Helen Suzman, the South African anti-apartheid activist, but she had been a magnificent Alexandra in the film *Nicholas and Alexandra* in which the cruel fate of the deposed Russian royal family was laid bare. As I waited alone for the doors of the lecture theatre to open I was joined by the great lady herself, who has since been made a dame of the British Empire. We soon became engrossed in discussing the art of performing in opera and drama before going our separate ways – she to work with the students while I looked on from the audience. You can imagine how flattered I was when she announced to the audience that there was an opera singer amongst them! It proved that after years in 'the business' I have always found that genuine stars are always most generous and gracious towards other artistes.

The passion I shared with the Italians for experimental musical adventure nearly brought an entrance audition to the Milan Conservatoire to a halt when the examiners were overwhelmed by the sound emanating from the well-built frame of one of my students. When an enthusiastic organist called Ezio asked me to teach him the basic elements of vocal technique to use in choral training I was only too delighted to oblige, especially as he was also a wonderful picture-framer and general handyman, only too willing to do odd jobs around my apartment. But singing lessons reached new heights and demands when he announced that he wanted to take singing as his second subject at the prestigious and competitive Milan Conservatoire. Ezio had not only a very husky speaking voice but vocal chords which produced a baritone quality that habitually transcended into a head tone resembling a falsetto. I was just about to give up when, in desperation, I decided to make this sound into one resembling a counter tenor, which, for those of you unfamiliar with such a voice, is like a male alto or female contralto. When I rang him with the good news, the poor man nearly expired with shock, propelling him to look up medical dictionaries to see if he could produce children. When I calmed him down and explained that I had worked with great counter tenors who had produced offspring, he agreed to sing 'Che Faro' from Gluck's *Orfeo*, since it was only for an audition to study at the conservatoire, and not a public performance. I was not present, but later that morning one of the professors rang me to inquire if the counter tenor who had bowled them over was one of my students. Apparently, they were curious to know who had taught him, until one of his colleagues suggested that it must be someone with an English background. After much discussion they decided that the person responsible for discovering such a sound could be none other than 'La Wright', since they assumed that I must have worked with great counter tenors like Alfred Deller and James Bowman during my days back in London, as a lucky member of the Ambrosian Singers. Later, Ezio's version of the events was rather different, for while he was in the middle of performing, one of the examiners approached him shouting *'Da dove viene?'* (Where does it come from?), with eyes transfixed, before inviting his colleagues to look down Ezio's throat to watch the strange female sound emerge from a robust, male body. It could only have happened in Italy.

The world of music mourned the death of a Chieftain in 2002 when the super-talented Ulster musician Derek Bell suddenly passed away, while I was left with wonderful memories of a lifelong friend, which I would like to share with you.

Derek and I first met when he was the oboist and I played second violin in a very select amateur orchestra comprised of adults ranging from the local resident magistrate to doctors and elite members of the local community. Rehearsals and musical get-togethers were held on a Saturday afternoon in the music room of Walden Lodge, my violin teacher's beautiful home on the outskirts of Newry. Mrs Henry was not only the most inspiring teacher I have ever had, but the kindest. To a young girl at the local grammar school Saturday was a magical day when I would strap my father's violin onto the back of my bike and ride out through the beautiful country lanes to the Lodge, where I also had piano lessons from her daughter Helene. On orchestral days I would have lunch with the family, who all lived together, while on lessons-only days, one of the family would bring in tea or freshly home-made bread and scones to refresh me after my morning ride. The Henrys were a complete orchestra in themselves: Mr Henry played the viola, Helene was a pianist, Lillian another violist, while Rodney, who also ran a market garden at Walden Lodge, was a gifted cellist and pianist. Away from home, Edith was an organist, while her other sister played the cello in the Halle Orchestra in Manchester. The Henrys not only were practising Christian Scientists but brought their message of peace and love into their musical soirees, and to those, like us, privileged enough to meet them. And so, it was in this magical setting that Derek and I learnt to love classical music and to mix with our peers. Years later he still remembered the moment that I made my 'debut' as an oratorio singer. It was during a rehearsal for Bach's *Christmas Oratorio* – when I wasn't required to play because I was on the back desk – that I couldn't resist humming the beautiful aria for contralto, 'Prepare Thyself Zion'. The sound must have drifted towards the conductor who suddenly stopped the orchestra to investigate where it was coming from. When I owned up he asked me to sing it before the rest of the orchestra, so that they would have an idea of the complete package – rather like the story about the professional cellist who played Bizet's *Carmen* every night from the orchestral pit, and decided to take a night off and join the audience where he discovered that there were some really good tunes up top.

Although we had played in the same orchestra, Derek was so wrapped up in his own musical thoughts that we never spoke – not even when I used to see him walking round the town on days home from boarding at the exclusive Campbell College in Belfast. But we were both kept informed of our mutual whereabouts through the grapevine of our amazing piano teacher, Dorothy Parke, who dreamed of the day when her two 'pets' would tie the knot!! Years later, when we eventually verbally communicated, Derek and I agreed that Dorothy was nothing short of a genius: it was she who decimated my dreams of becoming a concert pianist when she decided that I would never make the grade because my hands were too small, but I 'might not make a bad wee singer'. Having taken her advice I was informed by my singing professor in London that I would never make the grade in that department either because my palate was too small, leaving me no other option than to find alternative techniques to overcome my musical impediments. In fact, my Viennese accompanist, Rainer Keuschnig, used to marvel at the way I could find my way round the keyboard 'the wrong way'!

Derek was into his second year at the Royal College of Music when I arrived at what was a most prestigious centre of musical output over the years. Not long after, I was joined by James Galway and the horn player Ian Harper, whose Ulster accent I updated after his years spent in England. But it was the distinguished British composer Herbert

Howells who was to cement my friendship with Derek, whereas with Jimmy and Ian the 'craic' was infectious and uninhibited. Dr Howells was especially fascinated with Ireland and its people and when I began composition lessons with him he made sure that Derek and I would have our lessons one after the other. To say that Derek – or George as he was known – was prolific during his time at college is an understatement: symphonies and works for all musical combinations just seemed to emerge out of nowhere. Having just composed a work for violin and piano he actually made up the accompaniment himself on stage at a college concert, while the violinist played his already completed part: the result was electrifying.

After we both completed our studies Derek returned to Belfast and played the harp in the BBC Northern Ireland Orchestra, before joining the famous traditional Irish group the Chieftains, which brought him the worldwide fame he so richly deserved. In the years that followed I joined the Ambrosian Singers after a spell teaching at Roedean, the famous girls' school outside Brighton, before an adventurous spell living in Italy, so that it would be some years before our paths would cross again. This took place after my eventual return to Ireland, when Derek and I were guests on Sean Rafferty's Christmas special edition when he was with Radio Ulster before joining the BBC in London. Over the intervening years my voice had become deeper, which intrigued Derek so much that day that it inspired him to write a special work for me with a range similar to that of Ella Fitzgerald, the legendary black singer. Just before he left for an American tour with the Chieftains he rang me with the exciting news that he had found a wonderful text from an Australian poet and was about to put the finishing touches to it during the trip. But it wasn't to be, for within a few weeks Derek's sudden death was announced, while what was to be his last composition could not be found amongst his possessions.

His funeral took place the following month in St Anne's Cathedral in Belfast. Since it was open to the general public I arrived early to secure a good seat. When the verger saw me he pointed out that the first two rows were reserved for family and friends only, while the rest of the seats were at my disposal. Suddenly, this lovely man recognised me, as he himself was an amateur singer and had been to a lieder recital which Derek and I had given decades before in the Ulster Folk Museum. To my embarrassment he headed off into the sanctuary and returned with the dean's wife who not only escorted me to the section reserved for the privileged but joined me later in the adjoining seat.

During that sad time many musicians were invited to pay their respects on radio programmes, while the general public expressed their surprise about my being left out of the tributes to him after such a long musical trip together: but my friendship with famous musicians and colleagues has been always genuine and personal, simply because they know that I have never used their names to boost my own ego. But the opportunity to pay tribute unexpectedly presented itself after a roving BBC interviewer with an English accent, who spotted me sitting alone in the cathedral, starting chatting to me about his enthusiasm for the beauty and atmosphere of a building which he loved so much. During our chat we began talking about Derek, whereupon he switched on his microphone so that I was able to give him all the information he needed. When he asked me what, in my opinion, Derek would leave behind, I said it would be the memory of a friend who, in my case, stood by me when the chips were down. After we had finished he told me that it would be on the news that evening, which I missed as I was on my way home from the wake; but I was thrilled when Radio Ulster repeated our chatty interview in their review of the year programme.

A call from my agent in Genoa heralded a gradual reunion with the Italian musical world, when, after an absence of seventeen years, I returned to that wonderful seaside port on Italy's divine Ligurian coast to join a wonderful team who needed my urgent assistance to coach English in their production of Benjamin Britten's *The Rape of Lucretia.* The music of this most celebrated of British composers is honoured and frequently performed in a country so associated with Verdi and Puccini, and during the three weeks I spent in Genoa two of his masterpieces were being rehearsed and performed simultaneously; our production of *The Rape of Lucretia* was in a smaller theatre, while *Death In Venice* was drawing enthusiastic audiences to the main Carlo Felice Theatre.

I first went to Genoa in the late 1970s to sing the role of the governess in Britten's *Turn of the Screw* in the old Teatro Margerita, after which

I was invited back to sing with my new voice of mezzo-soprano in Mahler's second symphony; but Teatro Carlo Felice, which in the intervening years had been rebuilt after being destroyed by fire, has to be seen to be believed. An imposing white building towering over Genoa, this wonderful theatre was furbished with all the facilities to show off opera at its best. Artist's need to relax and rehearse in opera houses and concert halls which are equipped with bathrooms, rehearsal studios and canteens, in contrast to the usual cramped and often shared dressing rooms, cold toilets and chaotic make-up corners which all have to be endured before facing the general public and critics. Teatro Carlo Felice not only has space in which to breathe but large excellent rehearsal rooms, as well as practice rooms where musicians can warm up and study their scores in private. Often I would wander into one of these rooms overlooking the port of Genoa to watch the cruise liners navigate their way through the harbour in the early evening, before returning to the nearby hotel to eat gorgeous local delicacies with the singers and members of our production team. Not only did it host those of us involved in both Britten operas but other musicians on tour, from the Chamber Youth orchestra of Europe to an American company performing the musical *Hair*. It reminded me of the time when I worked as a film extra in Rome in the *The Statue*, in which I took part in an embarrassing extract from *Hair* alongside the great David Niven.

Over the years the expansion of modern technology and Facebook have strengthened my ties with Italy, keeping us all in daily touch with each other. But Genoa and Venice have a special place in my heart, as these two cities have given me opportunities and love which singers can only dream of. Even as I write this book, I am indulged with videos from Carlo Napoli in Genoa of great opera productions and singers from the past, as well as the beauty of Venice by day and night, and pictures of mouth-watering dishes lovingly prepared by my publishers in Milan for all to see.

Living in Rome in the *dolce vita* era in the 1970s was surreal – rather like a scene out of the film *Roman Holiday*, starring Gregory Peck and Audrey Hepburn, at that time married to a doctor and living in Rome; indeed she could often be seen – just like everyone else – shopping in the fashionable quarter of the city. The film industry was flourishing with big stars like Elizabeth Taylor, Richard Burton, Sophia Loren and Gina Lollobrigida descending on the world's most famous city to make epic films. Even I was snapped up by an American film agent as an extra, appearing in films directed by William Wilder starring David Niven and Jack Lemmon. Unfortunately, that all came to an end after I was asked, and declined, to appear as a German tourist in a nudist camp which was to be premiered in Venice, where I was beginning to establish myself as a contemporary music specialist at that idyllic city's Teatro La Fenice and the Biennale. There were parties galore and invitations were generously spread amongst Rome's thriving foreign community and the many embassies, whose splendid buildings and grounds still provide such luxurious settings for elaborate functions.

When my friend, the English mezzo-soprano Anna Reynolds, suggested that I should rent her apartment in the exciting quarter of Trastevere, I couldn't wait to move and embrace its somewhat bohemian atmosphere, full of artists, composers and singers from abroad whom I had already met professionally. To say that our flat was unique is an understatement. A studio flat in a turret would be an apt description, perched above more opulent apartments which were owned by some very distinguished residents, while, in contrast, it felt like I was living in bohemian Paris performing the role of the pathetic Mimi in Puccini's opera *La Bohème*. But this was unmistakably Rome, overlooking the River Tiber with views stretching from the Circus Maximus and Colosseum to the Sabine hills, from which a chilly winter wind gives Roman women the chance to show off their superb mink coats. Not only was I within easy reach of St Peter's and the Vatican, where, as an illegal guide, I showed tourists round the Sistine Chapel and its adjoining museum, but within walking distance of Piazza Venezia. On Sunday mornings I would waken to the sounds of church bells ringing from surrounding churches, and those of the beautiful Santa Maria in Cosmedin, opposite the Bocca della Verità – the grotesque bearded face with a gaping slot – featured in the film *Roman Holiday*. Surrounded by all this Roman culture and history was my combined bathroom and kitchen, which intrigued those who dined or lunched at number 1 Via Ripense. As one ventured into this bizarre room the wash hand basin – which served both as a kitchen sink and for washing one's person – was on the left beside a bidet – a continental requisite which was indispensable to one's personal hygiene, not to mention its use as a receptacle for rinsing out saucepans and draining vegetables. To the right, opposite the loo, was an ancient shower in a doughnut-shaped basin, while beside it was the fridge, on top of which were two gas rings from which meals were miraculously cooked and served, courtesy of a Dutch oven – a round ceramic cooking pot with a tight-fitting lid. From the opposite end of the apartment I looked down on the swimming pool adjoining the apartment of the brilliant Canadian-born photographer Roloff Beny, which he allowed his close neighbours and friends to use during his frequent absences abroad. When the Shah of Persia – now Iran – was in power Roloff made frequent trips to Tehran to stay with him and his wife, the beautiful Empress Farah Diba: his photographs of their coronation were spectacular and appeared in one of his many books about the country he loved so much. One evening he invited me down to his apartment to help him and his publisher select a photograph for the cover of his latest book on Persia, which I thought was such a touching gesture. Like so many great artistes Roloff treated everyone with respect, irrespective of class, and indeed, when he suddenly passed away, this was a characteristic that the self-styled Irish baron Brian De Breffny referred to in his touching obituary.

Both Roloff and Brian often joined us merry gang of fans on a Saturday night in Michael Aspinall's flat, just off the main Via del Corso, where we were entertained to opera as it has surely never been performed before. Michael, a Mancunian who never lost his accent, self-deprecatingly described himself as a 'counter tenor with a terrible voice' which he used to impersonate prima donnas, dressed up as a musical drag queen. Behind this mask there was nothing about the human voice which escaped his incredible vocal skills as a lecturer and teacher, having – like myself – done the rounds of singing teachers, until we wisely decided to rescue our own voices and careers. As a close friend and colleague, I always listened to Michael's blunt Lancastrian opinion on my own technique – or lack of it – for without a cast-iron one, survival as a professional singer can be short lived. When my Italian publishers invited him to write a brilliant article in *Musica* magazine to promote *La Wright* – the Italian translation of *The Rise and Fall of a La Scala Diva,*

Michael couldn't resist reminding my friends in Rome how a famous poet nearly met his end one Christmas night after taking a mouthful of my sherry trifle!

None of us in the foreign community in Rome at that time will ever forget the wonderful Christmas we spent together when we were unable to get home to spend it with our families. The impromptu fun began on Christmas Eve when I held a wine and cheese party before we set off to celebrate midnight mass and welcome in Christmas Day. Since the Dutch oven could not accommodate my turkey I asked my lovely baker round the corner to cook it for me, much to the amusement of his Italian customers, who, as turkey is not on their festive menu, gasped as I paid frequent visits to plaster packets of margarine over the huge bird. On Christmas night I, along with my own guests, were invited to my friend Jack Buckley's apartment at the top of a long flight of stairs in a palace adjoining the famous Piazza Venezia. It so happened that I had a left-over, untouched sherry trifle from my lunch party which I put in a plastic carrier bag to contribute to the party, unaware that Maria, Via Ripense's adored cleaner, had already used the bag to accommodate some spare German currency she found while 'distributing the dirt' in my flat. Somehow these coins must have found their way into the trifle on the journey, so that there was no one more horrified and surprised than me when Jack's poet friend nearly choked on a pfennig! What was even more shocking was that my Irish friend Michael, to whom you are about to be introduced, said, 'You naughty girl!' He firmly believed that I had done it on purpose.

I first met Michael Fitzgerald when I held an Irish passport and needed to contact the Irish embassy in Rome where his skills as a diplomat were well known. He certainly oozed Irish charm and, having quickly resolved my problem, was so friendly that I felt that I could confide in him that I was an Ulster Protestant, which he already knew from the Irish grapevine in Trastevere, where he lived. When he confessed that he too came from Northern Ireland, even though we didn't 'dig with the same foot', I realised that we had much in common, especially as he appeared to be such a cultured man. You can imagine my surprise when I saw his name on the communal post box at No 1 Via Ripense that we were not only neighbours but that he lived in the flat directly below me.

But it wasn't until I ran out of water, as my flat was *abusivo* – illegal in Italian, and I appeared at his door with a bucket to beg some that our paths again crossed. It also gave me an opportunity to apologise for the noise and weird sounds coming from upstairs that must have driven him berserk, especially when I got last-minute calls to deputise for an indisposed singer and was forced to spend an entire evening 'getting it into the voice', when all Michael wanted to do was read the *Belfast Telegraph* – the death columns of which we would read together, over a gin and tonic, to see if anyone we both knew from our part of the world was dead. After one very tough assignment, which drove even me to distraction, Michael looked so tired the following morning that the ambassador said, 'Has the Warrenpoint Warbler been at it again?' Since then the name of my home town and I became inextricably linked in the Irish community both at home and abroad.

But one afternoon Michael couldn't believe his ears when he heard a wondrous, magical sound drifting down to him from above. I had met Rolf Björling when he was studying with our mutual teacher, Debora Fambri. Like us all, Rolf was always searching for how to get the best out of his voice and when he asked the maestra – as she was affectionately known to her adoring flock – if he could contact me to give him some advice, she readily agreed, as even she was mesmerised by the 'music' which I brought to my lesson and the way I negotiated my vocal chords around it. When he arrived I was having my own problems studying Turandot's massive 'In Questa Reggia' from Puccini's eponymous opera, so that the score just happened to be lying on the piano. I shall never know what made me open it at that most famous of all arias, 'Nessun Dorma', but I did, telling Rolf to forget all about technique and just sing – whereupon, the Björling 'sound' and the God-given voice he had inherited from his father just poured out. That evening, Michael mentioned that if he hadn't known that Jussi Björling was dead he could have sworn that he was in my studio that afternoon. 'He is dead,' I informed him. 'That was his son!'

Clare O'Flaherty and I became friends when she was posted to Rome by the Department of Foreign Affairs in Dublin. It wasn't long before she became part of our merry group, helping us to cope with the trials and tribulations of everyday life and – where I was concerned – providing for my old age as a freelance musician. Everything about Clare was graced with elegance, from her tastefully furnished apartment to the chic clothes she bought from shops everywhere from her favourite La Fayette boutique in Paris to Rome's Via Condotti. She was obviously intended for diplomatic stardom: not only did she represent Ireland at the United Nations in Geneva but, in the ambassador's absence in Washington, she attended White House functions as chargé d'affaires during the George W. Bush administration. Soon after, she was appointed Irish ambassador to Finland. To our great sorrow, Clare was never able to fulfil that dream, or live to see her own old age, as she was cruelly struck down in her prime by motor neurone disease.

The first signs of her incurable illness became obvious when her speech became slurred as she was approaching the end of her stay in Washington. As there was no improvement on her return to Dublin to prepare for her Finnish appointment, her friends became increasingly worried, most of all Michael Fitzgerald, who, like me, had already returned from Italy to live in our native land. Since she appeared to be her usual elegant self, she couldn't have had a stroke, nor could it have been due to excessive drinking, as Clare had always been the one to reprimand our group after a liquid night out at Michael's favourite restaurant, just off Rome's Circus Maximus.

It was he – remembering my telling him about curing my own stammer and my breathing method for speech therapy – who arranged a meeting over lunch at the Conrad Hilton Hotel in Dublin – our favourite 'watering hole' for get-togethers. It was an enormous challenge for me as I was unsure if my unorthodox method would work, but, since I had successfully experimented with stroke sufferers, I immediately put my plan into action. Clare was sitting on the other side of the table to Michael and me, and after an hour of enduring the relentless pressure I imposed on her, she smiled and said, 'I can SPEAK.'

'Yes, you can,' Michael replied, choking back tears.

From then on, she rang me every evening at 5 p.m. when she would recite W. B. Yeats' beautiful poem 'The Lake Isle of Innisfree' to strengthen the throat muscles, which, unknown to us at that time, were not active. When I was free I would go to Dublin where we continued our 'lessons' over lunch at one of her favourite restaurants or visit works of art, about which she was passionate. As her appointment for Finland became imminent we were able – helped by warm-ups before meeting those in charge – to persuade the Department of Foreign Affairs to postpone her departure for Helsinki; but tragically, motor neurone disease was finally diagnosed and Clare died two years later on 11 September 2004.

Because I was not a specialised speech therapist, I wouldn't accept remuneration from her, but towards the end of our time together we had lunch at the beautiful Avoca Centre in her native County Wicklow, before browsing round its elegant shop. When I happened to spy a gorgeous poncho coat in cashmere and wool, Clare made me try it on, insisting that I should accept it as a gift. I still treasure it and keep it for special occasions, when I know it will be admired as something very special.

Writing began to invigorate me in a way that singing failed to do, possibly because the physical demands of performing and practising drains one of energy; but this was different as I basked in creating my own scripts instead of having to interpret the thoughts of those – how ever great they might be – who might not have agreed with my rendition of what they had conceived. Through this heaven-sent medium I was able to reveal the more gregarious side of my personality which I had been forced to hide from public view while earning my living as a serious singer. I was warned about this by a conductor colleague who reprimanded a lady after she enquired if I took my light-hearted banter onto the stage; he told her that one of the main reasons we did so many concerts together was that I was truly dedicated to my career and kept that side of my personality for dinner after the concert, when we could all relax and unwind after the serious business had been completed.

In spite of my eventually being recognised as a solo singer, it never brought me the same buzz as ensemble singing and the wonderful time spent with the Ambrosian Singers – Ambrosiani in Italian – back in the good old days in London. When the dashing Florentine composer Paolo Renosto introduced me to Nuova Consonanz – new sounds – I worked with a group of new composers who experimented with new sounds and ideas, with me as their 'guinea pig'. The patron of this extraordinary group was the distinguished Italian composer Count Giacinto Scelsi, who wrote French surrealist poetry and was a friend of Jean Cocteau and

Virginia Woolf. Count Scelsi was connected to distinguished composers all over the world, but centred his own compositions around one pitch. He was also a lavish host and entertained those of us privileged to know him in his beautiful house overlooking the Forum.

Musicus Concentus was an elegant ensemble from Florence, mostly made up from members of the Maggio Musicale orchestra and run by the pianist Alessandro Specchi, husband of Maria Tipo, the equally brilliant Italian pianist. Most of the concerts I performed with them involved the music of Luigi Dallapiccola, who lived in an apartment on Via Roma, not far from the Ponte Vecchio. When we were summoned to appear before the great maestro, we would make sure that we assembled not before the appointed moment of arrival, but immediately on the dot – a habit he inherited from the days when he studied with the great Schoenberg in Vienna. usually stayed in the Pensione Annalena and – rather like the film *A Room with a View* – I would find members of the ensemble on the same floor emerging from hidden corners to join me as we rang the bell, bang on the appointed hour, before being summoned to his great presence – although he was minute in stature.

The gregarious I solisti di Roma and I seemed to attract conductors with inflated egos like magnets. I first met this fantastically gifted group when I was called in at the last minute to replace an indisposed mezzo-soprano colleague at the Filarmonica Romana's venue at Teatro Olimpico. The French conductor simply refused to discuss the speed or work with me, preferring to read his *Le Monde* newspaper in his coffee break, leaving me in a state of bewilderment and trepidation as countdown to the evening concert loomed. When we eventually got together before a very distinguished audience, he set such a fast speed that I could hardly catch my breath. It was then that the leader, whom I knew well, whispered under his breath, 'Get it together and we will follow you.' From then onwards everything settled down and we gave the wonderful Hugo Wolf aria, arranged by Stravinsky, the treatment it rightly deserved. Unfortunately, the conductor was so incensed with rage that I was barred from French radio until he retired.

The next time I met up with this superb group of musicians was in Como, where we were to perform a new work under the baton of a young, inexperienced Dutch conductor, who happened to have indulged in a 'drop of the hard stuff' to calm his nerves. After a disastrous rehearsal, the group's leader decided that (with only a few hours to spare) we should put plan B into action to prevent a catastrophic concert. The only problem was that we had nowhere to rehearse: the only available room was mine in a hotel buzzing with tourists. As I arrived with my group of men, the receptionist turned a blind eye as he continued to welcome guests to the strangest of sounds echoing down the stairs from my bedroom. Eventually, we all emerged, having used my bathroom, as a changing room, and made our way to the beautiful Villa Olmo by the lake, by which time our conductor was in no state to stand up, let alone conduct. Once again, I got the blame for undermining his authority, and quite rightly so, but another conductor friend did not appreciate a phone call at 3 a.m. from a drunken colleague with the news that I had ruined his career.

It was Peter Keuschnig, the conductor of the Ensemble Kontrapunckte, who discovered the potential and chemistry to form a lieder duo between his brother Rainer and myself. When they gave a concert at Rome's Filarmonica Romana with me as soloist, he purposely included an Alban Berg aria for piano and voice, which he knew would bring the house down. From that evening to the present day, we have given many wonderful lieder recitals centred around the Viennese school of music, in which Rainer is an expert. Much of our work was centred around the Venice/Veneto region, so that it was easy for Rainer to catch the train from Vienna or for us to meet up in Milan, where I lived at that time. Nevertheless, wherever we went, our concerts attracted many young girls, who just had to get a glimpse of Rainer in his 'tails', which he preferred to wear instead of the customary dinner jacket.

The Ensemble Garbarino was another elegant outfit, under the direction of the distinguished Italian clarinettist Guiseppe Garbarino. He presented such an elegant style while playing that his breath control was phenomenal, especially in the Mozart Clarinet Concerto, which he insisted on playing without a conductor so that no one could inhibit his breath control. I learnt so much from touring as the only soloist with this group of musicians drawn from the principal Milan orchestras. Unfortunately, Guiseppe's generosity in refusing to take an Italian rival on a tour of Scandinavia and choosing me instead, led that particular soprano and her fellow soprano-in-mischief to implement measures to ensure that I could no longer work and live in Italy.

If I had to choose one from any of these wonderful groups, surely it must be Teatro Musica, who excelled in living musical theatre, experimenting with and performing avant-garde works without inhibition. I first met its director, Marcello Panni, when I performed four interesting songs composed by him in the foyer of the Rome Opera. It was a short but sweet encounter which was to herald many more exciting musical adventures together, including a very avant-garde work by a rather eccentric German composer, for which Marcello had persuaded a Spanish priest from the Vatican to join the merry group of myself and a rich actress at the luxurious seaside resort of Porto Santo Stefano, where Marcello had rented a villa for the summer. After spending an idyllic week amongst the rich and famous, and seeing how the 'other half lived', we were ready to go to the Biennale in Venice, where I was required to tell the audience – in English – not to worry that the show was nearly over!!

But the concert to end all concerts was when I was the singing narrator in a beautifully illustrated piece about birds by the artistically talented Sicilian composer Francesco Pennisi. A saloon in a palazzo on the Grand Canal before a distinguished gathering was the setting for this elegant event, which turned into an evening of spontaneous laughter when, at the last minute, Marcello sent over to the nearby Teatro La Fenice to borrow their Papagena bird costume from their *Magic Flute* production. Within minutes, I was zipped into this costume of feathers to face these dignitaries, unaware that a huge tail was waving behind me: by the time the show was over uninhibited laughter had taken over as everyone rolled over into the aisles. It certainly was a night to remember and one which I shall never live down. Marcello's mother was equally adventurous in casting me in a character role and defied all our critics when she chose me to sing the role of the sorceress in *Dido and Aeneas* with the great Jessye Norman as Dido. Both she and that other great patron of the arts, Alba Buitoni, had a unique way of persuading their internationally famous artistes to come for modest fees, just for the honour of singing at the Filarmonica Romana and Amici Della Musica, Perugia, where Signora Buitoni was immensely kind to me when she paired me off with the brilliant Neapolitan pianist Bruno Canino, before he joined up with the American violinist Itzhak Perlman.

My research and pre-publication for my magnum opus brought back so much joy into my life, as I relived and shared precious memories with those whom I held dear, that I wanted to shout it from the roof tops. Unfortunately, I landed on the wrong one when I chose my local GP – not the most cheerful of souls – who, unknown to me, was an ex-psychologist who was more interested in listening to the dark side of her patients' lives and the melancholic Irish stories which made them happy. As she was a 'blow-in' to the town she didn't realise that I was a native, still remembered by those of my generation as the tennis-mad teenager whose voice could be heard all over the shore as I practised my scales for the competitions and scholarships which would eventually take me to La Scala, Milan.

Never in my wildest nightmare could I have foreseen the horrendous repercussions which would change my life after I told her that I was in the process of finishing a book about the wonderful people I had met and famous venues in which I had sung. It had never occurred to me that she not only thought I had taken leave of my senses, but that someone like me, with such an opinion of themselves, and suffering from such vivid hallucinations to boot, must be suffering from bipolar disorder, of which this behaviour is a symptom. Later I attributed my instincts to my imagination working overtime and put it out of my mind; but I was soon to discover that the world of music had changed since my innocent days of glory, and that my career had found its way into a celebrity-driven and personality-obsessed society.

I grew up in an Ireland where one was compelled – for the sake of appearances and fear of the priests – to attend one's place of worship on a regular basis and bow down to the professional classes of whom one was subconsciously in awe. Doctors were treated like gods whose opinions one never doubted – nor had we reason to. Our family GP was a certain Dr Malcolm who not only was cherished and trusted by those in his care but became a close family friend and godfather to my nephew. A product of the land, Malcolm was the son of an apple farmer and a wonderful down-to-earth character without airs and graces, who was the ideal doctor for the everyday man and woman in a rural community.

He developed a special rapport with my mother who, like his own, had been an English teacher and fanatically instilled an everlasting use of good grammar into her flock, making them totally intolerant of those whose pronouns, adjectives and use of tenses didn't live up to their expectations. To say that Malcolm didn't suffer fools gladly would be an understatement: he certainly was not afraid to use his eloquent literary style to write letters to lofty consultants on his patients' behalf. When one of the recipients rang him to complain about the letter he received from one of these frightened patients Malcolm replied, 'I know; I wrote it and she signed it!' When the same gentleman successfully operated on my mother, Malcolm was expecting a huge clash of personality, but was disappointed when my mother described her consultant as a true gentleman, while he, in turn, thanked Malcolm for presenting him with a great lady.

But it was with the farming community that Malcolm came into his own, when he would attend wakes and enjoy the flow of Irish whiskey and yarns which he loved so much. After one of these evenings, which rather overran, Malcolm was at a loss for words when he had to take his leave of the corpse and the bereaved husband, who spared him the embarrassment of thanking him for a 'lovely evening' by saying, 'Och, doctor, isn't it a pity we couldn't have kept her another day!'

When I won the Associated Board Scholarship to the Royal College of Music he begged my parents not to let me go, as I was still under age; indeed Malcolm wasn't the only one who felt that I wouldn't be able to cope with the financial insecurity of such an unstable profession. Of course they were right, but my parents refused to listen, declaring that it was my life – not theirs – as well as fulfilling all their hopes and joys after the sacrifices they had made to make my dreams come true. Nevertheless, Malcolm and his lovely wife Olga became my greatest supporters, although they were not concert and opera enthusiasts. Eventually I begged Malcolm not to come to concerts where I could view him from the platform – bored to tears – counting how much per minute it had cost him to bring his friends to hear me.

Tragically my lovely career and wonderful memories were cut short on a balmy May evening in 2006 by my GP while I was out walking and basking in glorious sunshine without a care in the world. She had obviously been to my home – as she was coming from that direction – and, from the determined expression on her face, was 'out to get me'. In what can only be described as a premeditated attempt to abduct me, I was bundled into her car to begin eight years of relentless mental torture and self-doubt, which temporarily robbed me of my health and all I had accomplished in my life.

# Scene 3

# Intervallo

Unaware that I was being inveigled into a bizarre conspiratorial medical set-up, I willingly allowed my GP to take my blood pressure in her surgery, just across the road from where I had been kidnapped. Why should I have doubted her? Accustomed to previous sane medical care at home and abroad I had no reason not to trust a doctor, who was bound by law to respect a patient's privacy; so when she told me that my blood pressure was so high that I needed urgent treatment, I succumbed and allowed her to drive me to hospital with only the clothes I stood up in, while more deserving patients were left behind in evening surgery while she sped off with a woman in the fullness of health. This medical operation had obviously been planned beforehand with military precision, since I was immediately taken up to a female medical ward without any preceding examination. By midnight I was heavily sedated but sufficiently conscious to recognise various friends, who, alerted by the GP, had gained access to my home to get some clothes. Next morning a 'kind nurse' led me gently past the nurses' reception desk where I overheard a Casanova-type doctor entertaining his adoring audience of lady nurses with an on-the-spot commentary on the 'famous Marjorie Wright' as she passed by.

Inside a pokey room a doctor was waiting to talk to me in hushed tones: not only was he to change my lovely life and career for ever, but make sure that I should not escape from his clutches as long as I lived within the boundaries of his regional health board. If I had known that he was a psychiatrist I would have fled, but throughout the medical traumas that lay ahead, I was to discover that information and anonymity were consistently denied me and I was kept within the boundaries of the 'system'. Since it was my first time in hospital, I was completely ignorant about patients' rights, but in that medical compound confidentiality was washed aside and widely discussed. By next day everyone knew that the 'local celeb' had bipolar disorder, except me!!

After a week I was discharged after I was summoned to the office of Dr A – the principal psychiatric protagonist in this medical *opera buffa* – who said how wonderful it had been to meet me and that he would be sending a lovely lady to my home to see how I was progressing. Initially I was taken in by everyone's kindness, but I was soon to discover that many of those treating mental patients use sweetness and charm as a cover-up. On my return home I continued with my normal life until I received a letter from the hospital containing a leaflet about bipolar disorder and the threat of being sectioned if the symptoms recurred. If the shock of being informed of an incorrect diagnosis through the post, after a week of being kept in the dark in hospital, was not enough, I had been given the worst sentence one can imagine: a prisoner of those in charge of one's mind who, through the use of potentially dangerous drugs, have it in their power to deprive others of the freedom to think for themselves.

At this point of the opera I would like to introduce you to my wonderful friend and saviour, Peregrine Butler-Yeats. Peregrine and I met frequently on buses (although he owned a vintage Mercedes) but never spoke, although we used to acknowledge each other with an odd nod or smile. He was obviously very distinguished and 'posh', but always greeted the wonderfully friendly bus drivers with grace and charm, while the elegantly coiffed lady passengers were always eager to claim his attention. Since we both happened to be pally with the same bus driver, I discovered that our friend Peregrine was a retired doctor of considerable prestige who had worked abroad and although he owned a house in Belfast, preferred to live near the yacht club along the coast, where he indulged in his passion for rowing, in which he had a distinguished record. He was also a life-member of the elite Leander Club in Henley-on-Thames, to which he later introduced yours truly after we became good friends.

One day in late spring I happened to be sitting in the front seat of the bus when, having greeted our driver friend, Peregrine suddenly turned round and asked me if I would be interested in the ticket he was unable to use for the Henley Royal Regatta. It broke the ice, and from that moment on, a lovely friendship – courtesy of Ulsterbus – began. Every time he saw me get on the regular one on which he used to travel he would warmly greet me and keep me a seat beside him, while the twenty-minute journey would pass like a shot as we discussed the music of Schumann and Mahler, which we both loved. He was so excited about the contents of my autobiography that when it was eventually published, not only was he was one of the first to order it, but read it over and over again. The appreciation he had of my writing and humour was to prove an invaluable source of comfort and support to me during the darkness which was about to engulf my life, for it transpired that Peregrine had not only been a doctor but a scientist, a consultant psychiatrist in Canada and a university professor in England, where he had also set up two psychiatric clinics. And so, when I rang him in a state of panic about the bipolar disorder pamphlet he was a tower of strength, reassuring me that – under English law, to which he was accustomed – the form would have to be signed by the next of kin and be passed by a magistrate before being put into practice. 'But the whole thing is preposterous,' he said. 'They are scaring the wits out of you – a happy, fun-loving person who couldn't possibly be bipolar: so put it behind you and get on with your life.'

Unfortunately, I was to discover later that the law in Northern Ireland is rather different to that in England, as it only takes two doctors to sign a form, without the authorisation of the next of kin. If I had realised that I had unwittingly fallen into the hands of a GP and her scheming consultant counterpart I would have been on the first plane out of Belfast to seek refuge in a safer environment. Having been presented with such a psychiatric phenomenon, these medics were not going to lose sight of a disillusioned opera singer who believed she had sung at La Scala, Milan, and written a book which, in their eyes, was a figment of her imagination. Even my own family had difficulty in believing me; as they were descended from a long line of medics and clergymen, there was no reason for them to question a doctor's diagnosis. The only signs of mental deficiencies in a family noted for its brain power were in my Aunt Eleanor who had the mental faculties of a child of eight. One would have expected her to have been hidden from sight because of the stigma her condition would generate but my grandparents kept her at home where she was able to live as a normal human being within her limitations. Although she was unable to participate in or understand adult conversation, she became a treasured member of our family, helping my grandmother and aunt with housework, as well as looking after her adored nephews whom she went across the fields to meet every day on their way home from school. When she died on the same day as her great-niece was born my cousin named his daughter after our aunt.

After the death of my wonderful parents, who had followed my career at home and abroad with an abundance of love and pride, there had been no reason for me to visit Ireland and the UK, where my relatives had carved out affluent careers and lifestyles for themselves. So when I was diagnosed with obvious symptoms of bipolar disorder – imagining I was someone else, spending money and laughing too much – I was left to face a life sentence of stigma and being doped into a state of submission and oblivion. To make matters worse, I was not informed that – according to patients' rights – it was not obligatory to attend an appointment with Dr A; but I was too scared not to attend his mental health clinic at the local 'crazy hospital'. Once again, I had given him the opportunity he was waiting for: as he lifted his eyes, which had been glued to my medical notes throughout the consultation, he eventually transferred them to his prescription pad to write down the first dose of anti-psychotic drugs which were to gradually transform me into a zombie. No wonder he was too ashamed to look me straight in the face.

It was during the summer months of 2006, just after the first dose of lethal drugs, that the pills began to kick in. A wonderful student had invited me to her lovely wedding in September and, although I felt strange and lethargic, I made the effort to attend; the joy on her face when she spied me in the congregation was a very poignant moment for me, as she never failed to arrive for a lesson without a posy of flowers, freshly picked from her garden. Already concerned townsfolk had noticed that I would pass them by without a glance or time for a 'bit of craic'. This lack of being cheerful was to prove costly when, not long after the wedding, I failed to act as my doctor's 'warm-up' to cheer up patients waiting alongside me in her surgery. In a state of defiance I pretended to look miserable, which had not gone unnoticed as she emerged from her consulting room to call a patient. By the time I left the surgery she was firmly convinced from the expression on my face and failure to 'perform' that I had bipolar disorder. Years later a consultant friend in England nearly choked on his dessert when I confessed over dinner what I had done. 'But you can't walk in to a surgery and come out with bipolar disorder: it develops over a period of time, not in a doctor's consulting room.' From that day forward, I had sealed my own fate by trying to be too smart: not only was I forced to take whatever I had already been prescribed for my genuine underactive thyroid but the latest bipolar drug, as well as other pills for God knows what, as by that stage I had lost count. Even the pharmacists who provided the lethal cocktail became alarmed as they watched my metamorphosis slowly unfold before their eyes.

By October I was completely unaware of any sense of feeling. Concerned friends tried to make me laugh or smile, but apparently I just looked blank. Then one morning the nurse assigned to my 'case' to act as chief whip and spy to Dr A happened to call. When she saw me she assumed I had taken an overdose, since I was quite delirious from the effects of a doctor's over-prescribed one. When she suggested that I should come off the new anti-psychotic drug, and go onto lithium I didn't question the implications, as I was so desperate by that stage that I would have tried anything; the only problem was that it would involve having to spend time in a psychiatric clinic, involving an estimated stay of two weeks to monitor the effects of such a strong drug. I would be free to roam around the fascinating cathedral city, which my mother so enjoyed during her first teaching job there, and to listen to the beautiful church music about which I am so passionate – not to mention autumnal walks in the splendid gardens of the compound. Because I was so desperate to address the situation I agreed to go on a voluntary basis. If I had known that lithium is an extremely potent drug with severe side effects I would never have consented, not that that would have made many difference, as I would have had been forced to do what I was told. On the other hand, there are many who would not be able to survive without it, so that, used in normal circumstances, it can be a life-saver, but as it has since been established that I never had bipolar disorder in the first place, it nearly cost me my life.

To ensure that my liver was in a fit state to absorb the lithium I was re-admitted to crazy hospital before being transferred to the clinic. On my previous visit there to control my 'high blood pressure' I had met a consultant with whom I had joked that if he could reduce it to normal in time for my book launch I would send him a signed copy. He really must have thought that I was bonkers for when we renewed our acquaintance before I was to be 'put away' he said, 'A spell in that place will soon fix you.' While researching mental experiences for this book I have spoken to many wonderful people who have managed to survive 'that place'. They told me that as they were discharged from that hell-hole doctors told them to go and kill themselves. Now that I too have had a taste of it, I believe them. Once my liver had been given the all clear I was 'loaded' into an ambulance while Dr Casanova and his admirers looked on. After an hour's drive to a building in the grounds of the psychiatric hospital I was unstrapped and taken by the elbow to a first-floor apartment, where I was 'delivered', like a parcel, into the waiting arms of a nurse. Once those doors were closed behind me there was no escape. I was in hell.

When I sang the role of Sancta Susanna in Hindemith's opera of that name at a concert in Turin for the Italian radio I was relieved not to be forced to perform it on the operatic stage, since the condemned saint was buried alive in a wall. Never in my worst nightmares could I have imagined being banged up in a home from hell, for my own good, into which I had been tempted and cajoled by doctors and a nurse. Stories of cruelty in Ireland have been well circulated throughout the world through films like *Song for a Raggy Boy*, in which a priest in charge of a reform home in Belfast beat a boy to death, and the 'Magdalen Sisters', who were unmercifully cruel to young girls who had 'sinned'. But the sister into whose care I was delivered was neither a wicked nun nor a priest, but a psychiatrically trained nurse who was to become both my nemesis and 'jailer'. On arrival I felt like a criminal as I was stripped of my jewellery and all my possessions, including my mobile phone, leaving me cut off from my family and all my friends. Although there was a communal phone in the hall, calls were not private and – in my case – were censored by Sister M, who, for some reason, hated my guts on impact because she assumed I was 'posh' and belonged to another class of which she disapproved.

Soon after my admittance I had to reveal details of my income which included a state allowance to which people in my age group were entitled. When Sister M pounced on this she immediately withdrew it on the grounds that it was illegal. Since I had no reason to challenge a woman in charge of such information I not only faced the possibility of being homeless but being prosecuted for benefit fraud. From that day forward both my physical and mental health plummeted, while all the joy I had derived from my career and the publication of my forthcoming book vanished in an instant. I always maintain that it only takes one to start a war: Sister M was about to fill the role in true Auschwitz tyrannical style. How such a woman was, and still is, employed by a mental health board in this day and age is enough to make one tremble.

Thirty-two men and women were accommodated in four wards on the same corridor of the apartment with eight beds in each one. At night one could hear men screaming from nightmares about losing their benefits and farms. The ladies were more docile, since I was to discover later that Ballyhoo House was not a psychiatric clinic but a rehabilitation centre for the elderly, where people who needed rest and care were well looked after and discharged fully restored to health. At least there were windows which I viewed as a means of escape, but they were too high to jump safely from, whereas those unfortunate enough to be shut up in 'that place' across the road, which we passed on our controlled crocodile walks, were holed up in wards without any. I only hope that they were spared the intense and deeply intrusive interrogation to which some, but not all, of us were subjected. One lady in the next ward to me frightened the wits out of me, as she had a wild look about her. As I slowly gained her confidence she told me that she had tried to drown herself in the river close to her home and was only saved by clinging onto a tree trunk, until the fire brigade and ambulances arrived on the scene. The reason for her attempted suicide was that she feared that she would be prosecuted for benefit fraud. After some days she revealed that she was receiving an allowance – similar to the one that I had been on the point of losing; but since her doctor had retired she assumed that she was no longer entitled to it and was receiving it illegally. When I told her that it would have automatically been passed on to his successor and that she had no need to worry, the joy and relief in her face said it all. Why couldn't her consultant, or anyone, have listened to her and put her mind at rest? The reason for this could be explained because the patients are so much in awe of doctors and men of the cloth who look down on them that they are too afraid to talk to them. But, in fairness, the majority of patients worshipped them and considered them to be the best. Ironically, I was to have an unexpectedly brief encounter with one of these 'worshipped' consultants later on in this soap opera.

By a stroke of luck my distant cousins lived within easy access to the hospital campus and, as well as being a source of great comfort and strength, were able to keep my frantically worried immediate family in England updated. Without them I would still be there, since only family members were allowed to remove patients beyond the boundaries of the hospital grounds. It was also a wonderful opportunity to get to know their children who had heard lots of stories about my wonderful childhood, but little about my lifestyle and career in England and Italy. Even today they tease me about hiding my light under a bushel, but that is the way I prefer to live my life, since I have long discovered that if you are good people will find you without (to quote a good Ulster expression) bumming and blowing.

As winter set in it became more difficult for friends and family to visit since visiting hours were restricted to evenings and weekends to enable us to take part in daily occupational therapy classes which included bingo, current affairs, quizzes and light exercises. I became quite good at bingo, in spite of the fact that the staff remarked that, because of my upper-class connections, I was obviously more familiar with a game of bridge! Little did they know that I hate games and am a social menace when it comes to playing cards. The current affairs classes were entrusted to a young carer who entertained us to the deaths column and recent atrocities from the local papers, while baking was in the hands of a charming lady who gave me the job of stirring the ingredients for the Christmas cake; in fact my marzipan was considered to be a great success. After I purposely messed up a plate by painting the wrong design I ceased to be so popular and was considered to be an upper-class moron. But what I dreaded most were the mornings, when I was summoned to the quiet room to be cross-examined daily by a young, inexperienced nurse who was assigned to report to Doctor A on my daily progress and behaviour. Since she had never been to a classical concert, let alone an opera, the situation became intolerable for both us. Finally, when we both became so distressed to the point that we were on the verge of collapse, I decided that it was time to call a halt to the torture it was causing to us both. On Dr A's weekly visit I asked him if he would allow me to use my own personal method of obliterating thoughts from my mind, which, ironically, is available today in my book *The Wright Way to Breathe*. By sheer good luck he fell for it: not only did it give me space but it accommodated his brainwashing game plan to stop me from thinking at all.

Throughout those endlessly long days, which started at 7 a.m. when we cleaned ourselves within the privacy of our cubicles in a kitchen washing-up basin, I began to meditate and became used to my own company. Once my morning interrogation stopped my health began to improve and, as a result, I felt more in control of the situation. Months later when I told Peregrine about pretending to be completely doped and brainwashed he congratulated me for outwitting the staff, while a friend who is a theatrical producer said that I had performed my greatest role to date; nevertheless, despite their support, it was one that I would easily have swopped for an on-stage rather than a real-life one.

As my weekly consultations with Dr A progressed I noticed that I was becoming an interesting subject for the students who were usually present. During a particularly interesting session, when Dr A – who repeatedly asked the same questions – inquired if life was worth living, one of them complimented me on a stunning performance. I replied that as I was a dramatic soprano in real life, and wanted to commit suicide, I would do it in style by going to Rome and jumping from Castel St Angelo into the River Tiber, resembling a scene from Puccini's *Tosca*! The overawed student became even more confused after I informed him that I was only doing my job, as, in real life, I was an authentic professional. 'What are you doing here?' he asked. 'You tell me,' I replied. Two years later that rhetoric was to be reiterated over and over again when Sister M and Dr A were to make another entrance on stage. In the meantime I even managed to convince this formidable woman that I was for real after I decided to try out my voice in the toilet, just to see if I still had one. When she heard the note resounding along the corridor she congratulated me on the power behind it, while, at the same time, relishing the thought that my talents would be of great service in the institution to which I would be eventually detained.

But it was not long before I was to have the last laugh in this war of attrition when, on one gloriously sunny morning, while happening to search my handbag for a missing pen, my hand picked up a piece of crumpled paper: it was the flyer for the cover of *The Rise and Fall of a La Scala Diva*, which my publishers had sent for my approval. Not only was it the proof that I needed, but the director Sandy Leung's brilliant idea to have all the photos of me on the front cover was the proof of the pudding, since there was no mistaking the identity of the author, whose name was Marjorie Wright. Those lovely carers and nurses who had been kind were over the moon for me, while the rest were forced to capitulate. Although this miraculous discovery did not have immediate effect, the entire atmosphere changed and I was no longer subjected to humiliation and the threat of facing a lifelong sentence in an institution. I still had to undergo supervision because my liver was not responding as it should to the lithium; it was also some time before I was to discover that liver and kidney damage were some of the side effects of this strong drug, but, at that stage, I was so relieved to know that I would eventually be let out of captivity – like an animal released into the wild – that I couldn't have cared less.

Unfortunately book signings and a launch had to be cancelled but in the meantime I was allowed to spend Christmas 2006 at the Wrights' old family home in Co. Monaghan, while my family, along with my publishers and a mighty band of supporters, had formed a united front to have *The Rise and Fall of a La Scala Diva* online and in the shops for Christmas. By the beginning of 2007 I was a free woman, ready to restore order out of chaos and move on to a new life and a new beginning.

My father with his treasured violin.

My mother when she taught in Doncaster.

My paternal grandparents.

Derek Bell with just some of the many instruments he played.
He was best known as the harpist of the Chieftains.

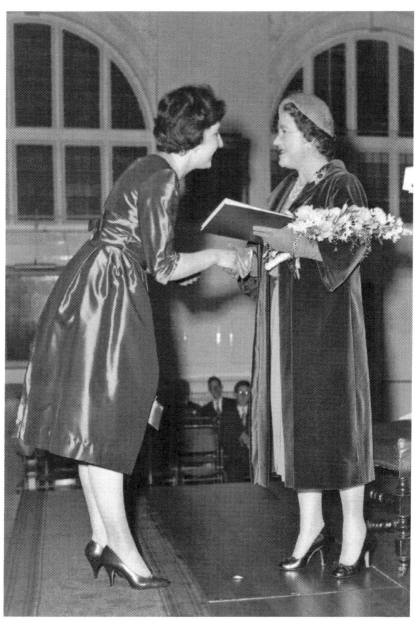

Being presented with the Clara Butt prize by the Queen Mother
at the Royal College of Music.

My mentor and guru – the Italian composer Luigi Dallapiccola.

As the mother in *The Prisoner* by Luigi Dallapiccola.

My singing teacher, Maestra Debora Fambri.

The famous Italian clarinettist Guiseppe Garbarino,
the director of Ensemble Garbarino.

# ACT II

# Scene 4

## The Scala Diva

Few musical contracts gave me the same thrill as signing one with a book publisher; yet if I hadn't experienced the ups and downs that inhabit the world of music I wouldn't have been able to gather together such live material with which to entertain the reader – or to extend my already fulfilled artistic adventure into the world of literature.

January 2007 heralded a new dawn and a fresh start. But I was to discover that promoting an autobiography was in sharp contrast to my first book, *How To Be A Bad Singer!*, which primarily dealt with singing technique, revealing nothing of the real me except to those in my most intimate inner circle. In contrast, *The Rise and Fall of a La Scala Diva* was like living in a goldfish bowl, with the general public delving into my private life, which, over many years, I had managed to keep separate from my professional one; in fact, I was considered to be a mysterious Irish girl who let those around her know what she wanted them to hear, and kept the rest to herself. And so, I gave myself a good talking to and faced up to the fact that if I were prepared to share my bizarre life with the general public I would have to deal with the consequences.

The local papers went overboard in their support and praise of a local author, whose years as a singer they had followed with warmth and great affection. One young journalist was so enthusiastic about my travelling from one country to another that she took a year off and bought a round-the-world ticket. A few weeks after I left the Ballyhoo clinic two old friends from different papers – whom I affectionately nicknamed 'The Paparazzi' – spent a day at my home, taking photographs and sharing stories which I had never revealed to them during all our years of banter and craic together. But it was my first venture to Belfast, soon after my release from hospital, which forced me to acknowledge that I had a fight on my hands and would have to call on all the acting tricks that I thought I had left behind at the stage door to create a camouflage for what was going on in my everyday life.

When an actor or singer portrays the work and personality of another person – like I did when I was Vittoria Colonna, Michelangelo's spiritual mistress – they have to discard the mantle once the job is done and move on to the next; but after a clever young journalist interviewed me for one of Ireland's widely read daily newspapers, I had to prepare myself to present different facades and characters in a real-life soap opera. Once the daily dose of lithium began to kick in, the side effect of muscle weakness began to take its toll, which the interviewer noticed and used to describe how I did not represent the typical opera singer he expected to meet, until I began to open up during our chat; given his expertise he would have brought out the best, and worst, of any artists lucky enough to interviewed by him. In spite of everything he devoted an entire page to the book in one of the paper's widely read Saturday editions and was one of the first to send it on its adventurous global journey from the city where I was born. BBC Northern Ireland was next in line to spread the news after I happened to bump into the mother-in-law of one of its most gifted presenters in my local supermarket. 'My son-in-law is looking for someone like you. I'll get him to call and see you next time he's down this way.' And so he did: *Days Like This* was an ingeniously devised programme lasting three minutes in which someone is asked to describe an incident which changed their life. I chose the one when I got my big break in Austria, while underestimating the appeal it would have to BBC Radio Ulster's regular listeners, not to mention the morale boost it gave to my self-confidence after I discovered that my own people were so interested in the world that I inhabit.

The story which unfolded that memorable Saturday morning on BBC Radio Ulster brought back vivid memories of an unexpected phone call I received from Switzerland to my home in Rome which was to change my life for ever: it was the break which every musician needs to point their career in the right direction when a colleague is forced to pull out of an engagement at the last minute and a replacement has to be found. Sadly, it so often happens in the music business that someone's bad luck turns into gold for another so that the show can go on. My English soprano friend had been so excited about being invited to sing at the impending world premiere of 'Commiato' by the Italian composer Luigi Dallapiccola that I feared the worst when the tone of her voice had an ominous ring to it. When she told me that she had been struck down by a virus while performing in Switzerland and was unable to travel to Austria, let alone sing, I knew what was coming next: could I do it? There and then, I had to book a flight to Vienna and pack my suitcase, without even seeing the score which, I was informed, was on its way by courier from Milan to Rome, allowing me time to study it on the plane. Nevertheless, it was a magnanimous gesture from one soprano to another, as we had both 'served our time' in the famous Ambrosian Singers and were accustomed to sight-reading difficult music with little rehearsal. I, in turn, was determined to do her proud on that October night in the snow near Graz in 1972. Working with the Ensemble Kontrapunckte can only bring out the best in soloists, as one automatically has to up one's game to keep up with their expertise. After that momentous evening, opportunities to work with other great composers and to sing at prestigious international venues presented themselves, making it the ideal story to tell on *Days Like This.*

It is sheer magic when the chemistry gels between two people, whether it be a conductor or an interviewer like Connor Garrett, whose knowledge of my subject made it so easy to chat to him and respond to his stimulating questions; but there was a fascinating twist to this popular programme when Connor's voice was edited out of the recorded interview, leaving me alone with the listener for three minutes to tell my tale.

By the spring of 2007 I was in such a state of vegetation that I realised that if I didn't set myself some challenges I would become a complete zombie. Towards the end of my singing career I had discovered that, after a period of time and repetitive practice, the muscles remember and – at an appointed moment – automatically take over control of one's performance – especially if, like me, one has problems memorising a score. During my time 'inside' in self-inflicted solitary confinement, I had trained my muscles to forget what I had just experienced, producing the obvious effect! And so, thinking big, I planned a book promotion to London where, years before, I had so enjoyed being my own sales rep, publishing my own home-produced edition of *How To Be A Bad Singer!* Even with the careful planning of my journey could I have foreseen what would happen as a result of my ever-increasing personality change under the influence of prescribed medication? Yet I survived, only because I was, once again, able to call on my acting and performing experience to pull the wool over others' eyes.

The fear of falling off footpaths into passing cars became so fanatically obsessive that I soon became familiar with those with flatter stones, while townsfolk where I lived were wonderfully helpful in opening doors to shops – even I didn't recognise the ones I knew; they just thought that I had risen above my station and didn't want to know them. I was fully aware that overcoming these obstacles en route to, and in, London would pose a problem, so, I booked a hotel near Marble Arch where I would be near familiar bus routes. Heathrow airport is always problematic – especially with a suitcase – because one has to go down escalators to reach the underground, so I booked a flight from Belfast to Gatwick airport which I knew well. From there, I found a lift which landed me right before the Gatwick Express train to Victoria station, where I caught a taxi to the hotel. Mingling with throngs of people after being enclosed for so long was overwhelming at first, but it gave me the opportunity to relish anonymity in a scrutiny-free environment. The hotel staff were particularly welcoming and were so impressed at having a writer as a guest that they bought copies of the book for me to sign.

With mounting confidence, I ventured to Hatchards, the famous royal booksellers in Piccadilly who had been the first to buy copies of *How To Be A Bad Singer!* There the buyer behind the counter recognised me and admonished me before a queue for interrupting the lunchtime rush: 'I have no time for sales reps! Come back at 3 o'clock.' To pass the time,

I went next door to Fortnum and Mason and had a rather expensive, but delicious, pasta before returning to the illustrious booksellers where I informed them – in my diva voice – that I was no longer a sales rep but had publishers to act on my behalf. In the end they were only too delighted to accept *HTBABS!*'s sibling before, as previously planned, I went to meet my friend Marcus outside Fortnum and Mason, where a rather different reception awaited me.

Marcus, originally from Belfast, is both a professional baritone and editor with a degree in English and Italian from Queens University, so when my Scottish friend Charles offered him a post teaching foreigners at his school in the northern Italian town of Piacenza, he lost no time in introducing him to someone from the same neck of the words. Marcus and I also grasped this heaven-sent opportunity to share stories and jokes from home which no one else could understand. Like Charles, he was passionate about classical music and opera, especially those mouth-watering open-air performances of *Aida* and *Turandot* at the arena in Verona. Along with our group of long-suffering friends, he also came to my own operatic appearances which weren't so traditional; at least he didn't fall asleep and was able to tell those who had nodded off to wake up in time for my next appearance on stage. But those fun days were but a memory, since we had both returned to the UK around the same time, although we still kept in regular touch, so that Marcus was well aware of my medical debacle back home. When he saw me the look of horror on his face said it all: there and then the full impact of what was happening hit me, while his immediate reaction was to pull me back into Fortnum and Mason and order some tea before he let rip.

'What have they done to you? It is your personality they are trying to change into a Marge we no longer recognise; if you don't do something about it you are going to lose yourself and everything you have worked for.'

'I don't know if I have the strength left to fight the medical hierarchy,' I replied.

'Well, you'd better put on your boxing gloves and get ready for battle,' he declared.

At last I had found someone who recognised that there was nothing wrong with me, instead of those who were afraid to admit it: and who could blame them, since it was my word against those in charge of human minds? When I criticise artistes who are consumed with their own importance Marcus reminds me about the grand exits I used to make from stage doors dressed in mink and 'acknowledging' my fans. Remembering this, I bestowed a diva farewell wave on him as I hailed a taxi outside the Ritz Hotel to begin the long journey back home to full recovery.

Over the spring and summer of that progressive year I concentrated on my health, walking as much as I could and keeping my mind alert by reading and listening to BBC Radio 4, to which I became addicted. By the autumn I felt ready to go to Milan and see my old friends, who were unaware of what had happened since my last visit. The blessing of being a writer and singer is that colleagues and friends in the profession assumed that I was touring, or busy writing and promoting my wares, so that when I flew into Linate airport I was full of confidence, since I knew it so well and was able to begin picking up the pieces in the company of those whom I trusted and loved.

As an avant-garde singer specialising in contemporary music, I was not only privileged to give many first performances of new works but to work with famous Italian publishers, like Suivini Zerboni and Casa Ricordi, famous for its publication of Puccini's wonderful music. It was through my collaboration with them that I met Luciana Pestalozza, a much-loved and valued member of their editorial staff, who was to become one of my closest friends and collaborators both on and off stage.

I first met her at an open-air concert in the gardens of the Accademia Filarmonica Romana in Rome at which I was performing a work published by Casa Ricordi. Accompanied by her young son Andrea – now a celebrated concert pianist and conductor – she approached me with her hand outstretched, announcing, '*Ciao, sono* Luciana' (Hello, I am Luciana). It was to be the first of many professional encounters when she would arrive on my doorstep with a bottle of Grappa to sustain me while I struggled to find a way round the difficult score which she had hidden behind her back.

I shall always remember her buzzing around La Scala, trying to calm down the cast, when I sang the role of Vittoria Colonna in *Nottetempo* by the flamboyant Italian composer Sylvano Bussotti, who was still writing the opera while we were rehearsing. When one of my colleagues was worried that he hadn't seen him around I told him that I, too, feared that he was still writing; sure enough the next morning Luciana would appear on the scene from Ricordi bearing packages for us to study at the last minute. With great respect to those great inventors of today's music, it was always a relief to sing Beethoven or Mahler who were beyond interfering at rehearsals, although Sylvano was a one-off dream, with a dry sense of humour which relieved the palpable tension which existed between my two soprano colleagues.

But it wasn't until I was with Luciana at the Biennale of contemporary music in Venice (where every September great composers and conductors, of whom I was totally in awe, would assemble) that I discovered her true identity: her late father was the violinist and teacher Michelangelo Abbado, her elder brother Marcello was the then head of the Milan Conservatoire, while her younger one just happened to be the world-famous conductor, the late Claudio Abbado. The Abbado-Pestalozza family were friends indeed when they took care of me after I broke my leg. When political innuendos made it impossible for me to remain in Italy it was Luciana who wisely advised me to leave my singing career at the level it had reached, and return to the UK. From my more secure environment I kept her up to date with tales from my 'downstairs' world of Mrs Mops and spare jobs back, while she remained 'upstairs' in Milan manoeuvring my return to work in my adopted country.

Over the years that had passed since our professional collaboration, Luciana had retired from Casa Ricordi and established Musica Milano – an organisation which presented modern music and composers' new works at prestigious concert venues throughout Milan. During my visit she brought me along to one of these events where I met Gabriele Bonomo, the representative of Suivini Zerboni and publisher of the late Luigi Dallapiccola's music. Having read my autobiography about the work I had done with the great maestro, he suggested having it translated into Italian by the adventurous Zecchini Editori, the publishers of the widely popular *Musica* magazine, who he was sure would be an ideal choice. Once again, Milan had delivered the goods. As my Aer Lingus plane dipped its wings in salute as it circled round the city before heading over the Alps, I decided that the time had come to defy those who had tried to remove me from those wonderful contacts I had just left behind. And so, next morning I took the first steps towards draining my body of toxic chemicals in an attempt to recapture the old me and the friends whom I thought I would never see again.

By the following spring I was back again in Milan, but not before help came from a most unexpected source. My long-time friend and neighbour Marie had suffered a stroke during my two months in Ballyhoo House and had been admitted to a care home about 10 minutes' walk from where we lived. Although she was psychically impaired, her mental faculties had lost nothing of their sharpness and powers of observation. And so, when I went to see her for the first time after my discharge from hospital, she immediately noticed that, although I was psychically intact, there was something which was not the same about me. 'What has happened to you, Marjorie?' she exclaimed. 'You didn't shout "Hello, Marie" in your usual happy voice.' When I told her that I had to speak in quiet tones around those who were ill, she still wasn't convinced by my explanation. Nevertheless, that someone who had known me so well and shared all the changes in my life should be worried about my behaviour gave me food for deep thought. And so, when I returned from Italy and told her that I was about to detox myself, a mischievous sparkle at the thought of becoming my partner in crime said it all.

Although Peregrine Butler-Yeats was bound by medical etiquette not to discuss the use of drugs, he advised me how to avoid a cold turkey reaction by gently weaning myself off lithium. Over a period of months, as I took a chip of each pill every evening, I felt as if I was coming out of an induced coma and returning to my normal self. Marie couldn't wait for my visits to hear about the effect our carefully devised plot was having on the general public, so when I returned from my first appearance at a family reunion and informed her that comments were made, such as 'but I see nothing wrong with her anyway; she looks alright to me!' she was chuffed to bits. Marie lived on for another two years – long enough to share the blossoming of the seeds she had help me sow. As her life came to a peaceful close, I happened to be walking past her care home when my instincts guided me inside. On recognising me, one of the lovely nurses personally conducted me up to her beautiful room overlooking the lough, where Marie lay totally at peace. As her daughter and I kept vigil by her bedside – reminiscing about old times and the mischief we got up to in our teens, she opened her eyes on recognising my voice and whispered my name before drifting back into a deep and final sleep. According to her family, that was the last word she said.

Immediately after I celebrated St Patrick's Day, I set off for Milan to meet my prospective publishers, with whom I had already established a warm relationship by email and phone. It was also the first time that Luciana and I had met since the death of our great friend Susie Park, wife of the never-to-be forgotten Italian composer Franco Donatoni. Susie, who was born in Dublin, was a descendant of Mungo Park, the Scottish surgeon and explorer, who discovered the River Niger in Central Africa. She had obviously inherited his adventurous genes, for, hidden behind her great natural beauty, the outwardly laid-back Susie was full of mischief. During her spell at the BBC's make-up department, she was prone to giving clients an 'extra dab' in the wrong place, among whom was the great Italian baritone Tito Gobbi, to whom she left her artistic trademark on his famous *Rigoletto* eye. She nearly left it on me, too – when I was on holiday at the Donatoni dacha near Pantelleria in Sicily – just before I was due to leave for Rome to sing the sorceress with Jessye Norman, in Purcell's *Dido and Aeneas.* As my hair had become so bleached in the hot sun, we decided to dye it a decent shade of blonde, and so we forthwith set out to the village supermarket to buy the ingredients, which Susie later applied as I sat on a stone ditch, reminiscent of Connemara in our native Ireland. What she didn't tell me was that we had bought the wrong sachet! Not only was I left with a mop of black hair but my sunburnt skin was the same colour as the new black bat-winged dress I had specially made for my role as a witch. On my return to Rome I was totally unprepared for the reception I received as I appeared on stage with my new 'accidental' makeover, as well as – what the critics described as – my new voice, singing as a mezzo soprano instead of my previous soprano one.

When, to our great sadness, Susie passed away in Milan, we decided that I would await the arrival of her ashes in Ireland instead of attending the thanksgiving service in the city's Anglican church, giving me the unique privilege of being the only one of our Italian group of friends to attend. Under blue skies and a hot sun, a small but intimate group of family and friends gathered at the exclusive yacht club at Howth to bid farewell to Susie. It was where she used to go sailing with her brother to the uninhabited island of Ireland's Eye, just north of Howth harbour, off the coast of County Dublin. I happened to be in the boat carrying the young vicar, who happened to be prone to seasickness; but the water was kind that day, allowing us to throw masses of red roses after Susie's ashes as she drifted out to sea. Then, to the sound of the island's rare species of seabirds singing and chirping in the background, we went sailing round the bay, before returning to the clubhouse. I shall never forget it.

The offices of Zecchini Editori are actually to the north of Milan in the small town of Varese, towards Lago Maggiore and the Swiss border. Surrounded by mountains and a beautiful lake, it provided an ideal setting in which to meet the fun people into whose musical family I was about to be adopted. After a warm greeting from the Zecchini brothers, Roberto and Paolo, I felt so at home that I immediately began to rattle on about myself, without realising that they had already done their research! Having been out of contact with the world of music for so long, I was totally overwhelmed when they showed me a copy of their own *Musica* magazine, featuring my name as part of the team which had won the Midem Prize for a CD from the archives at the Cannes Festival in 2008. They obviously knew more about me than I did!! But their trump card was yet to come: after Zecchini's promotions manager, Nicola Catto, had read *La Scala Diva* he was the obvious choice to translate it into Italian. Like his father before him, he had spent two years in Dublin perfecting his English to such a point that he was able to interpret both the Irish spirit and humour, as well as the 'gift of the gab', which I had wanted to portray. I already had a sample of this at our historic meeting in Varese when he fell about laughing at my casual remarks while, at the same time, quoting passages from my book from memory. What I was totally unprepared for was the constant flow of hilarious emails between us through which we formed a great friendship and collaboration, more about which you shall hear as my story unfolds.

Next morning I flew back to Dublin, on top of the world, making sure that I got – what had by then become – my lucky seat on the Aer

Lingus plane. And why not? *The Rise and Fall of a La Scala Diva* was about to be transformed into *La Wright. Una cantante fuori dal commune*, while I had just been accepted back into the world of music at the highest level. Not even in our wildest dreams could the Zecchinis and I have written the script for all the joy and camaraderie that wonderful day in Varese was to bring us.

My parents were so passionate about sport that listening and watching it nearly ruled our lives. To say that my father was addicted to football, a passion he handed down to his grandson, would be an understatement; yet, while honeymooning in Scotland, he laid aside his dislike of golf and cricket to succumb to my mother's dream of visiting St Andrew's golf links, near Dundee, where his cousin was not only a doctor, but a member of the famous club. He must have been love-struck to endure the slow pace of the sport, but agreed to accompany his bride to the links – St Andrews being a male-only establishment – where they were to meet up with his cousin. Eventually when my mother spied a bald man with a big nose swinging a golf club with his left hand, she recognised him at once.

'But you have never met him!' said my father.

'No, but I would know a Wright anywhere.' I, too, have inherited the family nose, while, being a left-handed hockey player, I was put between the goalposts out of harm's way.

Saturdays in our house were totally given over to football, which my mother loathed. Since TV was in its infancy we were spared the agony of watching *Match of the Day* and afternoon league football, giving us the freedom of moving about as long as we didn't speak – quite an achievement for a man living in a house with three feisty women. As the TV menu grew more appetising it was rugby which suited my family's combined zest for speed and excitement, as we waited with bated breath for those tries, conversions and last-minute penalty kicks to decide whether Ireland would win or lose. When they lost by a narrow margin my father would call them 'the victorious losers'; when they were overpowered by their opponents but managed to get a meagre try or a penalty, he would say, ' At least that has taken the bad look off it.' Years after his death one of his football entourage told me that he encouraged his mates to boo the opposite side to put them off their stride. I didn't know whether to laugh or hide my head in shame.

In the 1940s Irish rugby was on a high, uniting north and south of the island in one big happy sporting family, and it remained so throughout the thirty years of conflict in the north. When other countries were too afraid to cross the Irish Sea the English team did, receiving a standing ovation from an appreciative crowd in Dublin, before the Irish proceeded to lick them. This wonderful gesture is still remembered in Irish rugby circles to this day. In the early days, sportsmen and women were not professionally rewarded like they are now and had to earn their living outside, leaving the game in the hands of an eclectic gathering of men, principally made up of clergymen, dentists and doctors from north and south of the border. Centre field was dominated by the extraordinary chemistry and speed between Jack Kyle, then a medical student, and Ernie Strathdee, at that time a Presbyterian minister. As 'Strathdee to Kyle' rang out from our radio commentator, we just knew that a try would result as Jack ran for the line, while we would be up and out of our chairs waving our arms in jubilation, before it was successfully converted by the 'Elusive Pimpernel' as Jack was called. And why? Because they couldn't catch him! In 1948 this victorious team won the Grand Slam, after which they reverted to victorious losing, until Ireland won it again in 2009. Eventually, Ernie Strathdee left the church and took up a post at Ulster Television before his tragically premature death.

Performing on live TV scares me to death, so that by the time I arrived at Ulster Television's headquarters to sing an aria at the end of the evening news bulletin I was trembling with nerves, until a charming man, introducing himself as Ernie Strathdee, escorted me into the canteen where he treated me to tea and cakes. Instead of saving my voice, I had no intention of missing out on an opportunity to laugh and chat with my rugby hero. When my pianist cousin, also a fan of his, arrived to accompany me he, too, joined in the fun, so that by the time our dreaded turn arrived we were so well warmed up that we gave of our best. Even to this day I have never conquered my fear of radio and TV interviews: in a recording there is a chance to repeat and edit a mishap, while in a live encounter what's done is done and there is no turning back.

Decades later, I was to meet his great friend and rugby partner, Jack Kyle, when I had the rare experience to view opera from the other side of the stage. Not since my college days, when we were given free tickets to visit the exclusive Glyndebourne opera house in Sussex, had I attended such a beautiful setting as that surrounding the stately home of Castle Ward, on the shores of Strangford Lough in County Down. Our host for the evening had lived in Italy for some years, immersing himself in the operatic culture and world of Puccini which he continued to nourish on his return to Ireland. When he read my autobiography he immediately got in touch with me as he recognised so many people that we both knew, including Simonetta Puccini, granddaughter of the great Giacomo Puccini. Simonetta and I became friends after a concert in Milan in which I sang and she narrated. Those present will never forget the St Patrick's night dinner party I gave in Milan when I entertained Simonetta, two sisters of two different world-famous conductors, the brave husband of one of them and a society hostess, who, at the last moment, decided to bring along her Irish setter dog, Rory, to take part in our patron saint's celebrations. Rory and I had already met at a posh dinner party at his grand house where guests were waited on by a maid and kitchen staff, so that my humble abode must have been quite a culture shock for him. Just before his grand entrance I had avoided taking the rubbish down two flights of stairs by hiding it in a bag behind the telephone table outside the room in which we were eating. So busy were we tucking into a meal of stuffed shoulder of lamb – chosen because I hadn't the nerve to cook Italian food before such great cooks – that we forgot about Rory, until Simonetta said, 'Where's Rory?' There he was, his huge red bulk spread out over the floor, enjoying the left-overs from the black bag, while Simonetta said, 'Oh well, it's his St Patrick's Day, too.'

Ideal weather makes all the difference to an open-air operatic setting, as well as providing ideal conditions for the drive from my home along the scenic route to Castle Ward; but before we arrived there the driver, who had been despatched to ferry me and an English opera director, informed us that he had another guest to pick up, before turning left into an avenue lined with rhododendrons in full bloom. You can imagine my reaction when I saw Jack Kyle climbing into the back of the car beside me! David Beckham could not have received a greater ovation before we all set off to enjoy a gloriously informal evening without the elitism associated with such occasions. Mind you, it was only the general rehearsal! In contrast to the luxurious theatre of Glyndebourne, productions at Castle Ward were held in a converted barn on the estate. As I sat in my comfortable seat on 'the other side of the fence' I marvelled at the way the artistes managed to produce such wonderful sounds in such restricted conditions, since the back of the stage appeared to be the only means of coming and going. It reminded me of the production of Dallapiccola's *Job* at Venice's Teatro La Fenice when I followed the tiny female producer's instructions to deliver Job's drastic plight to the audience out front, while, at the same time, attempting to manoeuvre my considerable frame through a hole at the back of the stage. After much screaming and shouting from both her and the conductor, I asked the desperate lady to try it out for herself, after which a larger hole was made in the false wall to allow me to deliver my oration without stumbling onto the stage and missing beats.

Our visit to Castle Ward took place just before Jack was due to leave for the Rugby World Cup in Paris, and to send him on his way the director brought a hamper of French wine, bread and cheese for the picnic lunch during the interval. As we began chatting I wasn't going to miss out on the opportunity to show off my knowledge of rugby to one of the greats. I, in turn, learnt that the mother of Johnny Wilkinson, England's current wearer of the coveted 10 shirt, had been born in the same hospital in Zambia where Jack had worked as a surgeon. A small world indeed. When I rang the Festival's director to thank him for the lovely evening, he, in turn, thanked me for talking about opera to Jack. I hadn't the courage to tell him that I had a great time talking about rugby! Unfortunately, Ireland lost in Paris that year, but they later reclaimed the Grand Slam title which Jack, Ernie and their mates had won decades earlier.

To avoid suspicion I still ordered my supply of lithium, yet in my heart I knew that the consequences would have to be faced and so I obediently attended a blood check-up to avoid suspicion, totally unprepared for the fracas it would cause. The final scene of the drama took place while

I was basking in early summer sunshine in my garden; but it was short lived after a BMW car drove up to my door with a very angry doctor aboard, ready to berate me for deceiving her after the blood tests unmasked the absence of lithium. As she marched me into my own home, I was able to call on the technique that I had acquired for facing auditioning panels and presenting a more serious image for conductors who had no time for diva histrionics. Because this was a side of me that my GP had not seen before she diagnosed it as a 'mood swing' in need of an immediate dose of lithium. Realising that there was no way out, I pretended to agree to continue the dreaded dosage. Once she had gone, I knew that urgent action had to be taken and that I would have to change GP; but this was easier said than done because local doctors had an unspoken code not to trespass on each other's territory.

Once again, help came from an unexpected source when my cleaning lady introduced me to her highly recommended doctor whose surgery was in the next town, allowing me the freedom to go out for a walk without being picked up by a medic. Before we amicably parted company, my lady doctor magnanimously agreed to write a diplomatic letter in my presence to Dr A explaining that my 'flamboyant good spirits' had returned as a result of coming off lithium. It freed me from both his clutches and sidekicks, as well as laying to rest an unfortunate interlude in my life; it also left me to settle down to enjoy a normal medical routine under my new doctor. During that time the subject of mental health or my detention in Ballyhoo House was never mentioned, so that I assumed that he was either too embarrassed to mention it, or was completely unaware of it.

By the summer of 2009 excitement was gathering pace at breathtaking speed between Ireland and Italy as *La Wright*, by means of computer skills and shared flamboyant spirits, gathered momentum. Not only were my Italian publishers witty and funny but they became the heaven-sent musical soul mates I needed at that time to restore my faith in music and the human race. Nicola became so immersed in my story that he paid a special visit to my home in Ireland to personally absorb the atmosphere of what he was translating. After he interviewed me over my kitchen table, he selected memorabilia to take back to Italy, before

I took him to lunch at my friends' beautiful hotel overlooking the sea. It so happened that they were expecting a wedding party later in the day, but when I told them that my Italian publisher was coming to visit, they pulled out all the stops and rolled out the red bridal carpet early in Nicola's honour. After the owners received us at the door, we were led to a special table overlooking the panoramic view, while one of the waiters, whom I knew well, personally attended to our every whim. Over lunch I tried to hide the shock I got when Nicola announced that the book would be out by October, in time for the Christmas rush: that balmy September day in the town where I belonged was to be the beginning of the excitement and happiness which enriched and restored the life which I had nearly lost, after *La Wright. Una cantante fuori dal commune,* emerged to an acclaimed fanfare.

# Scene 5

# Marco, the Lion King

When I mention Marco's name my girlfriends imagine that he is my latest toy boy: He is none other than the prestigious Leone d'Argento, who represents the most romantic of cities and is all mine; so that it is no wonder that I love to see their reaction when they eventually meet him and are left speechless! To crown all, the manner in which he entered my life was so surreal that even I was left in a state of disbelief as to how it had all transpired in the first place.

It all began when I received an email from Nicola Catto announcing that the book was ready and telling me to indulge in a bottle of bubbly; forgetting that it only takes a few glasses to send me into orbit I decided to succumb and buy a bottle of champagne, which I brought with me to a friend's house with an already well-stocked cellar. After we had drunk a few bottles of its vintage wine my friends suggested that I should stay the night, but I insisted on calling a taxi so that I could sleep off the after effects of the liquid evening in my own bed once I had checked my emails. Noticing that there was one from my publishers I decided to leave replying to it until I was in a more sober state; what I didn't know was that I had automatically sent an empty reply to their extraordinary news that I had just been awarded the Leone d'Oro. When the Zecchinis received my nonchalant reaction to such news the following morning, they could only assume that, while attempting to type out the strange email, I had been taken to the nearest hospital in a state of shock; but before taking further action, they phoned my home, where, making a lame excuse that I had just returned from Dublin, I had sufficiently recovered from my hangover to join in the excitement which this wonderful accolade had generated around their office.

The person who made all this possible was Renzo Stevanato, the great Venetian bass and colleague, who, apart from being the president of the Mario del Monaco Association, is a huge force in promoting Venetian culture and the wonderful events, including the famous Carnival, which take place annually in that paradise. By sheer coincidence my Italian editors had just published a biography on the life of Mario del Monaco, one of the greatest Italian tenors of the twentieth century, renowned not only for his great operatic roles but as a fine teacher who produced great singers, of whom Renzo was one. And so, when he heard about *La Wright*, he offered to hold the book presentation in Mario del Monaco's apartment in my beloved Venice, where I had taken part in so many wonderful operas and concerts at the famous Teatro La Fenice, as well as the Biennale, for which the city is artistically well known worldwide. What puzzled me was why I had been awarded an accolade which I assumed was usually presented to actors at the climax to an international film festival. And so, I headed down the street to the Café Piazza to consult Oswaldo, the handsome owner of our local café, who served up and personally cooked mouth-watering Italian dishes and coffee, surrounded by pictures of all the landmarks with which I was so familiar from his native Rome. I was especially drawn to the one of the Roman Forum, as it reminded me of my spell as an illegal guide when I conducted tourists around it, courtesy of the *Guide Bleu*. Although he spoke perfect English, I unashamedly used Oswaldo to keep up my Italian and to impress curious customers. In the meantime, another email was waiting for me when I got back home with the news that all had changed: instead of the Leone d'Oro, I was to be presented with the Leone d'Argento. It certainly seemed more feasible, since it is given to film producers, or in acknowledgement of career achievements. Nevertheless, it provided a golden opportunity for my friends to remind me that if I had accepted, instead of refusing, a small part at the Venice Film Festival as a naked

German tourist in a nudist camp I might have been a strong contestant for the Leone d'Oro!

With only weeks to prepare for the launch, it was full steam ahead. Only an Italian production could have generated such excitement; it brought back all the wonderful nerve-racking moments leading up to the first night in an Italian opera house, when order is restored out of chaos and adrenaline flows. This great occasion was to take place at the cultural association's Christmas party for which I was invited to contribute a half-hour recital; considering that my singing career had been jeopardised by medical advisers, unused to patients who earned their living by means of their God-given voices, I had nothing to lose: and so, I started to vocalise and restored Gustav Mahler's heavenly 'Rückert-Lieder' to a voice that I thought I would never use again. To strengthen the link between the countries responsible for bestowing such an accolade on me as the Leone d'Argento, I included some of my favourite Irish folk songs.

I usually like to accompany myself at the piano, as it gives me complete freedom to adjust and judge audience reaction, but even I knew my limitations and decided to leave it to a more accomplished accompanist to perform Mahler before such a distinguished and knowledgeable audience. The problem was where to find a professional pianist at short notice with whom I could rehearse! My long-term duo partner, Rainer Keuschnig, lived in Vienna, my concert pianist cousin was heavily booked up, while I was too busy coping with interviews and travel arrangements to leave base. When Nicola suggested that he would play the Mahler I jumped at the idea as we would have time in Venice to rehearse, as well as cementing our author and translator relationship. What the poor man didn't know was that, although I might have given the impression of being a docile author, I am a holy terror to work with as a singer! Nevertheless, his own moment of fame came when one of my local journalists was so overcome by anticipation of the forthcoming concert in Venice that he wrote that Nicola Catto was giving a recital of Irish folk songs accompanied by Gustav Mahler at the piano! I wasn't even mentioned. And so, on the first Friday in December 2009, I set off with my merry band of supporters at the crack of dawn to board a Ryanair flight to Treviso, near Venice. I was absolutely livid at having to pay 200 euros in excess baggage, which was more than the fare; but then, if one is travelling with 'diva' luggage, it goes with the territory.

By evening, friends had arrived from Rome and England. Some managed to find rooms in my hotel near St Mark's Square, while others either stayed with friends or in adjacent hotels, enabling us to meet up and enjoy the exceptionally delicious food in the restaurant at my hotel. By Sunday, there was still no sign of Nicola as he wasn't able to leave Milan; but I wasn't unnecessarily worried as I we had 'rehearsed' by email. I was relieved when he managed to get a train on Monday morning which arrived just before the press conference at the Mario del Monaco residence, leaving us time to get our act together, have lunch and then rest before the early evening Christmas party; but it didn't quite turn out like that, as the press conference lasted for nearly two hours, leaving us just enough time to rush back to the hotel on foot in the rain – as there are only water taxis in Venice – and grab some food to sustain us through the challenge ahead.

After I threw my evening attire into a bag, we headed back in the rain to our venue, only to discover that there were people setting up chairs and preparing for the after-concert reception. Once I had donned my evening dress in Mario del Monaco's bathroom, I applied some make-up while Nicola practised on the grand piano with me whispering instructions to save my singing voice. Suddenly he warmed up by playing 'Oh Danny Boy', which he loved and had persuaded me to include in the programme. In it he had managed to capture the warmth and style needed for Mahler; 'Put your love of "Danny Boy" into Mahler,' I shouted over the background noise coming from the kitchen: mightily relieved I then realised that there was no need for further rehearsal because we had just established our game plan – meaning that we knew that all we had to do was deliver and everything would be fine. Even the heralded arrival of Rainer – the other half of my lieder duo, who had come all the way from Vienna to be with us – did not inhibit our performance, although afterwards, Nicola declared that he was a saint to have put up with me for so many years. What he didn't know was that the Viennese maestro would never have let me get away with the liberties that I took with the Mahler; in fact, he later said I was like a rabbit, digging its way out of a hole!! But he did, however, receive a standing ovation in recognition of his huge contribution towards my life achievement award and all the wonderful recitals we had performed in the Veneto region.

I had expected to meet Marco at the reception at the end of the evening but, lo and behold, I had just sat down to accompany myself in my first Irish folk song when suddenly, the tall frame of Renzo Stevanato appeared bearing the most wonderful piece of silver that I have seen. I was so overcome that I vaguely remember a dignitary presenting me with a majestic silver lion with eagle's wings, its left paw poised in magnificence over the gospel according to St Mark; that is why I call him Marco (Mark in English) the Lion King, aloft on his 'throne' of marble. His presence on top of the piano, in his beautiful purple box lined with silk, set the scene for the most unforgettable moment in my entire singing career.

Mahler's 'Ich bin Der Welt' must be one of the most beautiful songs ever written, reminding me of the pathos of his 5th symphony, which in which we all indulged in the film *Death in Venice*; to imagine that I was singing my heart out only forty minutes by water bus to the Lido where it was shot on location made it even more poignant. As I stood there while Nicola played the beautiful ending to the song, immobile and transfixed, all the trauma of the previous years melted into oblivion as I was truly metamorphosed into a reborn diva – the title of this book and its Italian translation, *La Diva Rinata*. Renzo was so over the moon with excitement that he wanted to sing – there and then – the famous duet 'La Ci Darem La Mano' from Mozart's *Don Giovanni*, but it was five years before we were able to fulfil that promise, owing to yet another unforeseen drama which was about to take over my life – sooner rather than later.

That night, as I was undressing in my hotel room, I felt an unusual sensation in my breast. My immediate reaction was to exclude all negative thoughts from my mind and assume that the lump I felt was a muscle I had pulled after the physical effort I had just applied to my body after such a long absence from the concert platform. I must have retreated into denial as my immediate reaction was to ignore the lump and pack my bags in readiness to leave the following day, not forgetting that I had a morning book signing in Venice's quaint Studium bookshop before a farewell lunch with those of my friends who still remained. On the flight back to Dublin that evening I casually mentioned to my travelling companion that I had pulled a muscle in my breast. Her face said it all: 'Surely God would not be so unkind as to rob you of all that you have fought for these last few years,' she said, before returning to the book she was reading.

What concerned me more was the controversy surrounding my supposed bipolar disorder: either I had it, or I hadn't, because I knew that I could not have coped with the Venetian festivities without medication if I was a victim of that horrible and debilitating illness: it simply didn't make sense. And so, a few days after my return to base I went to see Dr Timothy – GP no. 2 in this medical soap – to finally lay the matter to rest – one way or another.

'Am I bipolar?' I asked.

'Yes,' he replied, 'it's the pills that are keeping it at bay.'

When I said, 'What pills?' he turned to the computer to discover that he had never prescribed lithium, as I had weaned myself off the drug months before registering with him. While he tried to contain his obvious anger he ordered immediate blood tests which, a few days later, arrived back negative. As a result, I was taken off all medication and declared a fit and healthy woman, to be set free, once again, to get on with the rest of my life. Before taking my leave, Doctor Timothy advised me to 'put it all behind me', which was easier said than done. After I had delicately asked his opinion on how I should cope with the unfair stigma and shame attached to an illness which I didn't even have, he said, 'Weave it into your funny books!' At last I had been given a positive diagnosis.

Hardly had I time to catch my breath than it was time to look towards the Milan launch of *La Wright*; such was the line-up of authors waiting for their books to be presented at Rizzoli, the famous Italian bookshop in the Galleria near La Scala opera house, that it was June before we eventually got a booking. In the meantime, invitations and interviews had to be arranged, in both Ireland and Italy, so that momentum was at fever pitch.

Since there was more time this time to arrange Irish publicity I was able to acknowledge those who had contributed so much to my career over the years, beginning with Radio Telefis Eireann (RTE), who were the first of many European radio stations to give me the opportunity to perform solo recitals for voice and piano. These engagements were a breath of fresh air as I was able to perform music which I loved – in preference to unpalatable assignments which I had to accept to keep the wolf away from the door. When I presented a work to RTE by an Italian composer, the great Rhoda Cahill, one of their brilliant accompanists, refused to play it and forthwith replaced it with Schumann's divine 'Frauenliebe und -leben'. Although I had never before laid eyes on it, once we got the gist of it, we sang and played our hearts out, aided and abetted by the brilliant engineer who was to record many other wonderful recitals and concerts in which I later took part.

I was to experience the same thrilling adventure with another RTE pianist, the wonderful Kitty O'Callaghan, who also happened to be organist at the quaint University Church, beside Dublin's famous Shelbourne Hotel, which was the magical setting a friend had chosen for her wedding. The bride had insisted that I should sing an all Bach programme, including his beautiful Wedding Cantata, in which I just wallowed; but when we approached the communion part of the wedding, Kitty turned round to me in the organ loft, where we were having a great time, to enquire what I was going to sing for that part of the mass.

'That's all I have been asked to do,' I said. 'My contribution is over.' There and then she dived into the music chest and brought out Caesar Frank's 'Panis Angelicus', which I had always longed to sing.

'But the bride hates it.'

'Blow the bride,' said Kitty, whose back straightened at the altar rails as we let rip. I don't think my friend ever forgave me for disrupting the tranquillity of her wedding, but to have an opportunity to perform with such a brilliant musician does not often come around and has to be grasped with both hands.

Great accompanists can either make or break an artiste. I had the great fortune to give recitals with the brilliant Neapolitan pianist Bruno Canino. He was a great favourite of the late Signora Alba Buitoni, the president of the Amici della Musica association in Perugia. It was she who suggested that I should team up with him to give a recital of Hugo Wolf's songs at one of her exclusive Sunday afternoon concerts. When Bruno arrived to rehearse at my home in Rome, he confessed that he hadn't had time to look at the music, but when we began to rehearse he was able to point out details which I had overlooked; by the time we arrived in Perugia, we were a real team. After Bruno went on to form a magical duo with the American violinist Itzhak Perlman, I teamed up on a permanent basis with Rainer Keuschnig. It was he who introduced me to music from the Viennese school of music, including Schoenberg, Berg, and the rarely heard songs of Alma Mahler – the controversial wife of Gustav. Through his work with the Vienna Philharmonic, Rainer insisted on making me sing Mahler with long breaths by not cutting the ends of phrases – a technique that wonderful orchestra uses to obtain that unmistakeably broad tone which makes their sound so easy to distinguish from other major orchestras. It is through his perseverance that I am still able to carry on singing, well past my sell-by date, as we made a pact that I would stop at the first sign of a wobble.

I inherited my love of Dublin from my mother, who studied there and embraced the culture of that city renowned for its saints and scholars. Many distinguished careers and great Irish names have emerged from the Feis Ceoil (the Irish equivalent of a Welsh Eisteddfod), where talent is nurtured and developed from an early age at the highest level. Amongst its most famous exports were the great tenor Count John McCormack and the writer James Joyce. According to legend, Joyce had the better voice, but could not sight-read as well as McCormack to win the Feis Ceoil's coveted gold medal. McCormack went on to study with the great Maestro Sabatini in Milan, who was a rare breed of teacher that didn't tamper with his students' natural voices, encouraging them to focus on the wonderful breath control for which the Irish tenor was famous – most notably in his wonderful recording of Mozart's 'Il Mio Tesoro' from *The Marriage of Figaro*.

But it wasn't just Dublin where the *Feis* – as Irish festivals are known – flourish, but throughout the whole country. My introduction to the stage, of which I was terrified – and still am – began when I won the under-twelve singing competition at our local one, although I was less scared sitting at piano competitions where I couldn't see the adjudicator or the audience; nevertheless, if it hadn't been for my cross-border musical upbringing I would never have won a piano scholarship which eventually paved the way for me to sing at La Scala, Milan. Many have reached great professional heights from the same musical environment, among whom are Sean Rafferty, of Radio 3 *In Tune* fame, and John Toal, both of whom have interviewed me on numerous occasions with the same ease as if we were chatting in our own natural habitat. Seamus Crimmins, another of our merry band of music makers from the same cultural nest, was the founder of RTE Lyric FM no less, producing top-quality music from all over the world, along with announcers who have the gift to involve and immerse the listener in details of the work being played, as well as the composer and its country of origin.

One of the greatest teachers and musicians Dublin produced in the late 19th century was Vincent O'Brien – not to be confused with the horse trainer! The links that I have established with those who were influenced by his great skills are considerable, including his son Oliver, whom I first met when I made my debut as a soprano soloist in Dublin when he was chorus master of Our Lady's Choral Society. Handel's *Messiah* is one of the highlights of the Society's season and when Oliver invited me to the O'Brien home for the audition, I was honoured to be shown around his father's memorabilia.

At the same time my parents and I enjoyed a close musical friendship with of one of Vincent O'Brien's most renowned pupils, Lillian McCardle-Trodden. A contralto from Newry with a God-given voice, she was given a welcome home usually accorded to the Down G.A. Football team on winning the All Ireland Championship, after she won the Golden Voice competition in London. Whenever I performed in Ireland, or was at home on holiday from the Royal College of Music, I always valued her expert opinion on my voice, since she was one of those rare teachers who had the gift of recognising the individual sound belonging to that particular person – and no one else. Mrs Trodden was also beautifully dressed with not a hair out of place, making her the perfect role model for her famous choir, The Dun Eimear Singers, whom she conducted with the same elegance and finesse that Vincent O'Brien achieved with his Palestrina Choir, still based at Dublin's Pro-Cathedral.

I shared many a chocolate marshmallow with her son Russell, also a talented musician and teacher, as we mischievously mimicked people whom we thought were a 'little above their station'. But to those who didn't know him well, Russell was a model of sobriety, always immaculately dressed in a smart suit and fancy waistcoat, even in the heat of summer. He was also a devout Catholic, opposed to the mass being celebrated in English, while bitterly criticising those unfortunate priests who did; nevertheless, we both shared an ecumenical love of Elgar's 'Dream of Gerontius', based on Cardinal Newman's poem, when the soul passes through purgatory on its way to heaven. As I kept vigil by his bedside as he peacefully passed away from cancer, I kept wondering what stage he had reached on his journey to meet the God in whom he so believed.

RTE certainly rose to the occasion when, a matter of weeks before the presentation of *La Wright* at Milan's famous, prestigious Rizzoli bookshop, they gave Marco and me a rousing send-off. As a regular fan of *The Afternoon Show* I was already an admirer of the cosy programme and knew that they would live up to my expectations; but when the great day arrived I was completely blown away by its energy and exhilaration. The show began on arrival at the reception desk when I was listed as 'La Scala Diva', instead of my own name. As everyone gathered to view the diva whom they assumed had just flown in from Milan they were amazed to meet a home-grown one who had just arrived at RTE'S impressive building on the outskirts of Dublin by public transport, courtesy of my O.A.P. free Ulsterbus pass. Since it was the last week before the end of the popular series, everyone was in festive spirits. The producers and I had already established a great rapport during their thorough research by phone and email, so that by the time we met we were well prepared for take-off; and what a blast it turned out to be. As I gobbled up the wonderful beef sausages in Guinness sauce for lunch, well-known faces in the canteen came up to introduce themselves, while the excited interviewer kept bursting in to upgrade her script with extra uplifting additions. By the time the red light was switched on, the party spirit was well under way, with the off-screen cameramen and the entire studio crew joining in on the fun. It was a day I shall never – nor want to – forget.

Although I was bursting with energy and good health I decided to have the pulled muscle in my breast investigated as a precautionary measure, and so my GP made an NHS appointment at the local hospital shortly before I was due to leave for the Milan book presentation. A visit to a Macmillan breast cancer centre is not the ideal way a woman wants to spend a morning, but nothing could have prepared me for the waiting room full of terrified women – some still in their teens – preparing themselves to confront the moment that everyone dreads. I personally felt as if I were sitting in a courtroom waiting for a jury to deliver a sentence. After we were each scanned we were ushered into another waiting centre outside the office of the male consultant. As the queue diminished I sat there as one by one these frightened women, full of despair, were comforted by waiting relatives or anxious friends as they came out of the consulting room. As the last lady left I was left alone, while the consultant arrogantly strutted round, casting ominous glances in my direction.

After a long wait, a nurse told to me to go to the canteen and return an hour later; at least it gave me time to ring a friend to come to the hospital and drive me home. In the meantime, kind young ladies at the reception desk brought me a pot of tea and lots of sugar to relieve the tension until, after the longest two hours of my life, I was finally ushered into the presence of a man in his late fifties, to whom I took an instant dislike. My greatest sympathy goes out to doctors, since there is no easy way to deliver bad news, but on that occasion, the manner in which mine was presented was brutal in the extreme. While two nurses held me down, this pompous man, with the authority of both judge and jury, read out my sentence: 'You have aggressive breast cancer; I shall have to remove your left breast, after which there will be no reconstruction procedure.' That was the day that my world crashed around me: not only had I been given a life sentence, but was left totally unprepared for the almighty battle I was about to wage against the merciless medical team who were about to destroy my hopes and dreams.

After the initial shock wore off, there was no option but to salvage what I could from the wreckage. Since the Milan presentation was but a few weeks away, my GP agreed that it would be wiser to go ahead with the arrangements, as cancelling the already organised event would cause even more stress and chaos. And so, having resigned myself to an uncertain future, I booked a flight to Milan so that my Italian legacy could be left to posterity. Once Mr B was informed about my decision he did everything within his power to prevent me setting out for Milan, a city renowned worldwide for its research and pioneering development in the field of oncology, and where I had influential contacts. A week before I was due to leave, I got a phone call from the hospital inviting me to meet him in his office for 'a wee chat'. As I waited to be called, his nurse warmly greeted me at the end of her shift, leaving me alone with a man who had others ideas in mind – far beyond the boundaries of what a consultant can legally enforce on a patient. After I was subjected to an over-enthusiastic examination, he handed me a form to read and sign, before leaving and returning to the room with such speed that I had little time to digest the contents. All I could remember was signing a consent form to have my breast and lymph glands removed, which is usually signed by the patient or next of kin immediately before an operation, and not before boarding a plane. By the time I was ready to leave for the airport I had made up my mind to put the breast cancer issue temporarily behind me and to enjoy every minute of what time was left to me with the people I loved.

Never in my life have I experienced such utter joy and fulfilment as when I saw *La Wright* and a poster with a rather flattering professional photo of myself as a young woman gazing out of the main window of Rizzoli. As I sat outside a posh coffee house in the Galleria overlooking the window with my book displayed for all to see, no one could have berated me for not thinking enough of myself. For someone who detests the blowing of one's own trumpet, I allowed myself to temporarily indulge in wondrous reality, so that by the time Nicola arrived carrying Marco in a pink plastic bag, my joy was complete. Marco had spent the time between the two Italian launches with my publishers, who had brought him back from Venice to their office in Varese for the rest of the staff to enjoy. From that moment of reunification, Marco was not only to steal the show, but take over my entire life.

When I arrived at the homely Euro Hotel where I always stay the staff couldn't believe that I was bringing the Leone d'Argento back to them after the presentation, as they had read all about the trophy in the press. As his safety presented a risk, it was initially decided to put him in a room in a quiet part of the hotel, but when he went on view and was so admired, he was taken away to remain in the hotel security vault until my departure for London.

Before I left, the staff helped me put sweaters around him in his pink bag to prevent him making his presence felt going through security, but he safely passed through the conveyor belt without a squeak to join me in the queue for the flight to London Gatwick. The only problem was the weight of the heavy marble base which I had to carry up the gangway, but when news spread about the prestigious passenger about to board the plane – not me – an Italian steward came down the steps to take him on board the aircraft and place him in a secure place in the luggage compartment above my seat. On arrival at Gatwick an official was summoned from the bottom of the gangway to carry Marco down the steps, before we both were loaded onto a buggy which conducted us past the other weary passengers from the flight who graciously waved to us as we sped by them on our way to the terminal building. In record time we were given VIP treatment through passport control, before being deposited at baggage reclaim and into the arms of my two nephews waiting outside to meet the new member of the family.

By coincidence, my great-niece was celebrating her eighteenth birthday that weekend in Surrey, allowing precious time to spend with my family; it also gave me the opportunity I needed to discuss my medical dilemma with them, as well as the feedback from my Milan trip when I was advised by a top man in the field of oncology to have a second opinion before allowing anyone to remove my breast and cut short my singing career. That weekend, with so much to lose, my family and I decided to seek another opinion in England with a reputable cancer specialist who would treat me as an individual and not according to what prestigious venues I had sung at; and so, out of courtesy, on my return to Ulster I rang both my GP and the consultant's secretary to tell them that I would no longer require their services. On receiving the news that he had dreaded, Mr B was not prepared to let the matter drop and immediately set out to take drastic steps beyond the boundaries of medical etiquette to remove my breast at all costs. It was then that I remembered my friend Peregrine Butler-Yeats telling me that opera singers and cabinet ministers are vital assets to enhance a doctor's list of patients, and that mine would not let me go without a fight. How his words of wisdom echoed in my ears when I was brought to justice for disobeying doctors' orders, with battle cries of no surrender waging on all fronts.

# Scene 6

## Intermezzo

The date 19 October 2010 will be for ever implanted in my memory: not only was it the anniversary of my father's death but the day on which unexpected guests from the local health authority turned up on my doorstep to trigger off two months of undercover operations, which – although they still remain an unsolved mystery – subsequently led to my deliverance out of the hands of the enemy. No opera libretto or plot that I know of resembles any of the scenes that followed because – other than myself – no one would have been able to invent such a script. And so, I leave it to you, dear reader, to decide whether it should be staged as a comic opera, or a 'whodunnit'. Since I had the star billing in this one-off soap, in which I had to imagine myself in every singing role imaginable, from Desdemona in Verdi's *Otello* to the pathetic character of Liu in Puccini's *Turandot*, this real-life opera would make a libretto fit for an Oscar, with all the clues pointing towards Mr B, the wicked surgeon, disguised as Scarpia in the same composer's *Tosca*. Before I proceed, I shall have to take you back to the day that I was left alone with Mr B in his hospital office without the presence of a nurse. During our conversation, I thought that he should be aware of the lethal amounts of anti-psychotic drugs to which my system had been exposed under the care of Dr A, the psychiatrist, who just happened to be his golfing mate. How could I, or indeed any patient, have known that by being honest and confiding in the very man whom I should have been able to trust, I had sealed my own fate. Not only did he vandalise my rights as a patient but used this as his chief weapon in this battle of medical chess, even after I had informed the hospital in late June, after my return from my book launch in Milan, that I no longer was his patient. So you can imagine my shock and indignation when I got a letter with details of admittance to have a mastectomy on my birthday, two days before 12 July, which is Orange day in N. Ireland. Obviously, it had been brought to his attention that there were important parades to attend, so that the operation was postponed for another week, by which time even the hospital staff were beginning to lose patience with this never-ending farce. It did, however, allow time for Mr B to catch up with Dr A, and compare notes. No doubt Mr B told him about the reluctant diva who left him stranded without a body to operate on, while Dr A must have realised that he had let loose a confused woman he hadn't seen or heard of for two years who still imagined she had sung at La Scala and written a book. How breast cancer and bipolar disorder can be related requires a massive stretch of the imagination, but the fact remains that these two cronies allegedly defied all the rules of medical etiquette to employ their mutual diagnosis, past and present – correct or incorrect – in retaliation against a woman who had the audacity to undermine their superiority and legally discharge herself from their registers.

Over the remaining summer months I decided to consult family doctors in England. Since Dr Timothy was socially involved with the two consultants, I decided to sever all connections and, if necessary, go to England where I would be treated individually and without social implications. In the meantime, I managed to persuade a practice nearby to take me on as a temporary patient in case of emergencies. As it happened it turned out to be the biggest and most momentous decision of my life, since it brought eight years of medical hell to a dramatic conclusion. What followed is unbelievable; so fasten your seat belts while I spill.

Towards the end of September I was surprised when, out of the blue, I got a phone call from Dr A's secretary asking me to make an appointment to see him. I Explained that I was no longer his patient and therefore saw no reason to contact a consultant whose department had no connection whatsoever with cancer. About a week later, this persistent man himself phoned me himself to discuss my cancer diagnosis, which was none of his business, although I offered to meet him on neutral territory in town; but he still insisted on seeing me within the hospital complex and left instructions to ring his secretary for an appointment. Once my suspicions were aroused, I contacted the hospital administration who assured me that there was no need to panic, as I had every right not to visit the hospital if I didn't wish to. But news travels fast in a small community, especially where so many doctors live in lovely surroundings where they can socialise and – like any other profession – catch up on the latest gossip. Indeed close friends of one doctor commiserated with me in the supermarket about the cancer debacle and said that, as a singer, I was doing the right thing in seeking an opinion in London at the Royal Marsden. Considering that I had only discussed the matter with a trusted friend and those close to me outside the community, I could only assume that my story had come from inside information.

Not long after, it was the turn of Dr A to take centre stage, when – completely out of the blue – he turned up at my home, along with his sidekick. Since I had no desire to talk on the doorstep, I had no option but to invite them in, leaving the door wide open for him to resume where he had left off in Ballyhoo House. When he asked me what speed my mind was pulsating I told him that it was ticking along so well that I had been to Venice and collected a trophy, pictures of which I showed him as proof of the pudding; unfortunately, Marco was still in Surrey at my nephew's home waiting for me to collect him, giving these obsessed men the impression that, once again, it was all in my mind and a figment of my imagination. A few days later my concerned neighbours saw two men acting suspiciously outside my house, dressed in suits and carrying briefcases. The following day, a doctor and a social worker rang my door bell as I was having lunch to carry me off – with no explanation – to spend a long weekend in hospital.

During the intervening years, Ballyhoo House had been closed down and the remaining crew transferred to a new building, virtually next door to the main hospital where Mr B was in charge of cancer patients. Having realised that he and Dr A were now neighbours in crime,

I told the driver that he had dropped me off at the wrong entrance, as I had cancer and not mental issues; but when I saw the reception committee which even the Duchess of Cambridge would have graciously acknowledged – minus the red carpet – I knew he had made no mistake. Those remaining from the nursing and caring staff from Ballyhoo House were genuinely excited to see me back with them, telling me to relax and enjoy my holiday weekend. Sister M was extremely cordial; no doubt she was relieved to know that I was back under her wing, albeit for a brief spell. Certainly, the new accommodation for mental health patients was like the Hilton, compared to Ballyhoo. On arrival I was taken to a bright room, overlooking a garden, with a bathroom equipped with everything one could wish for; a mystery fan had even left a special gift to welcome me, which continued throughout my stay, so that I would know that I was not alone in a loveless environment. What I found most harrowing was that the majority of patients were so mentally incapacitated that they were unaware of their beautiful surroundings and rooms, not to mention the scrumptious food, which was to die for – if you will excuse the pun. It caused me so much pain watching them being fed at meal times, that even Sister M took pity on me and sent meals to me in a cosy TV room; perhaps she had a hidden soft side to her after all.

I did make friends though with two most delightful ladies who, like me, were able to fend for themselves. One of them was truly beautiful with a great sense of humour and fell apart laughing at my jokes when we got together. When I asked the reason why she was there, in seemingly robust health, she said that it was because she had tried to rescue her son from his wicked ways by reading him chapters from the Bible; even though he didn't live with her, he had her put away for a few days at a time because he objected to her reading him such trash. There and then, we devised a plot to play him at his own game. I told her not to mention God, and, after what he had done to her, he wasn't worth saving anyway. What did and still does concern me is the indiscriminate amount of power given to doctors and social workers to have someone sectioned, without the authorisation of a judge or magistrate; even the wishes and feelings of the next of kin are often not taken into account.

But this was not the case with my other lovely lady friend who had a shake in her hand, and to whom I became close after she recognised my loving and caring cousin who visited me and just happened to be her doctor's wife. When she told me about the kindness shown to her by my cousin's doctor father-in-law when her 19-year-old daughter died of cancer, I told her that her daughter would never die, as she would be reunited with her in heaven; this is something in which I firmly believe, and I pray that any bereaved person reading my story may be comforted by it. It also had a happy ending, as there was such an immediate change in her condition that not only did her doctor congratulate me but has since taken a keen family interest in all my projects.

I first became aware that something was up when on the second – and supposedly the last – night of my holiday I saw Dr A hurrying down the corridor outside the residents' sitting-room. When I casually asked one of the patients if it was a normal procedure for the doctor to visit on a Friday night he said that he only did so in an emergency, otherwise he only visited once a week. It wasn't long before I discovered that I was the reason for his being there, after I was taken to a quiet room to wait until I was called. Suddenly the door burst open to reveal Dr A's boss, whom I recognised from the former Ballyhoo House but had had the good fortune to never meet. Once he had introduced himself I was handed a sheet of papers and asked to sign them – 'just to cover themselves' – without being given a chance to read them. Mission completed, he then left me, only to return after a short interval to ask me if I thought I was special. 'No,' I replied. 'I am an opera singer.'

That was the last I heard of Mr B and Dr A until a week later, during Dr A's routine visit. Expecting to check out on the Saturday, I asked a kind male nurse if I could go home as promised, but he said, 'Do nothing; remain calm and continue with the blinder you are playing. You are a magnificent actress and keep it up, because it is working.' That evening, a special form of indoor entertainment was put on for my benefit, with nurses bringing in photos of their weddings and children to share with me. Although there was a festive atmosphere, I was still left to ponder my fate and the reason for my being kept there for no specific reason. Considering that I had been diagnosed with unattended serious breast cancer, being feted as of guest honour at a party in a psychiatric unit could only have belonged to a farce. The next day, a lovely Florence Nightingale – who had been an angel to me in Ballyhoo House – told me that there was deep concern about the state of an under-active thyroid disorder, the treatment for which had been discontinued after the former blood tests ordered by Dr Timothy had returned negative instead of positive. She gave up her Sunday to spend the day in the laboratory to restore the necessary medication which, like a diabetic, an under-active sufferer needs to survive; if not taken, acute tiredness sets in. By Monday 23 October, the honeymoon was over. By that stage, I was desperate and terrified in case the delay would cause the big C word to spread. Fortunately, I had been able to keep my mobile and laptop so that I was able to enlist outside help. I had word sent to my temporary GP to have me moved to a medical ward in the adjoining general hospital, for I had realised that having my breast removed was preferable to mental torture and mind games. I have since been informed by members of staff, who kept in touch, that since mental and physical records are completely separate Mr B might not even have been aware of how close I was to his operating table.

Even the doctors and staff were at a loss during the first week of my 'holiday' – for there was no obvious reason for my being detained there. One intelligent doctor suggested a liver scan, after he asked me why I was occupying a bed when there was nothing wrong with my mental state. 'I don't know,' I said. 'You tell me.'

When I came to life after a young lady doctor started a normal conversation with me about my books, she immediately told me to be quiet as the reason for my being detained was that I was an active woman in need of rest. By this stage, I had played all the roles I could imagine, from being quiet to cheerful; the only one I avoided was that of a madwoman, as I knew I was being slowly manipulated by this cleverly briefed staff into believing that I was. A week later I was called before the jury who had finally reached its verdict, to be found guilty, or not guilty. When Dr A – once again, surrounded by unfamiliar sidekicks – asked if I knew the reason for my being there I said, 'You tell me.'

'You are being assessed to see if you are mentally capable of refusing an operation for breast cancer.' While I sat there, numb and speechless, he went on to say that, because of a new system of care, they were sending me home, where I would be assessed under their new scheme: in other words, I was being let out on bail. When I informed the jury that, in my opinion, I couldn't have bipolar disorder, as I did not take to my bed or suffer bouts of depression, they all agreed; yet Dr A was only too eager to administer a course of pills to prevent me from being too gregarious and high spirited. What sort of composure they expected from a woman suffering from diagnosed breast cancer I shall never know; but by that stage I had learnt to keep my mouth shut or I would never escape from their clutches.

The following day, I was allowed home; but this time round, I had no way out, because the social workers who appeared at random on my doorstep were sent to keep a watchful eye on me and make sure that I was back on enforced anti-psychotic pills. Nevertheless, I was relieved to resume my plan to attend to the more serious issue of my cancer diagnosis, which hadn't been mentioned during the interview or throughout my stay. How doctors with whom I had had no previous contact, or I had only met briefly on one occasion, could have had any indication of what I was like in my private or professional life will always remain a mystery. The only indication of any personal involvement between us was when Dr A congratulated me in their presence on how much he had enjoyed reading my book, which had been given to him for the sole purpose of catching up on my past history, and discovering the reason for my outgoing personality and artistic achievements.

As soon as I got home, my incandescent solicitor was ready to declare war and sue the health board, but all I wanted was to be alone, away from the madding crowd, who, unknown to me, had no intention of conceding defeat. Dr A's army lost no time in introducing themselves after they continued to invade the sanctuary of my home to monitor my movements. I can only assume that the way to manipulate people's minds and coax them into obeying must be part of mental training, because, by then, my instincts had trained me into the art of submission and playing them at their own game. In any other situation, I would have enjoyed the company of the social workers assigned to my case, as they were genuinely kind and charming, but, to quote them, they were only doing their job. Even the sympathetic man in charge acknowledged and apologised for keeping me under 'house arrest'. By then I was beginning to empathise with the Burmese opposition politician Aung San Sui Kyi: she was detained in her own home for expressing a political opinion, while I was being punished for exercising my just rights as a patient. But all was not lost, for just as I was about to make an early morning escape to catch the first plane out of Ireland, a massive undercover rescue operation was about to reveal the strength of Ireland's girl power.

Obviously alarmed by the medial records transferred to my new practice, Patricia, my feisty and glamorous current GP, must have panicked when she read them, for immediately I got home, she got in touch to arrange an immediate appointment with a lady consultant in whom she had faith. Her obvious trust in this woman reassured me so much that I instinctively agreed to return to the same hospital's Macmillan unit on a day which didn't host Mr B's clinic. At last, the time had arrived to experience the love and work carried on by those dedicated to cancer care. Plucking up enough courage to go through that dreaded door for the second time, I sat down amongst women calmly reading magazines and without the fear that I had experienced on my previous visit. When a young lady dressed in a surgical uniform approached me, introducing herself as Sandy, my new consultant, I knew that I was in good hands from the word go. Having decided to ignore the previous diagnosis and start from scratch, I met her again later that morning, after the same team of radiographers had completed their scans. They welcomed me back with open arms and hugs with the news that, after my previous visit, they had looked up my book on Amazon and bought copies to give as Christmas presents.

The result was so positive that I treated myself to a sigh of relief. Over the Christmas period, I was to experiment with a drug which, hopefully, would keep the cancer at bay until my next appointment two months later. But I still hadn't reached the summit of the mountain, as there was more to climb. On the Friday before this appointment, a brave young hospital secretary risked her job to warn me that Mr B had found out that I had a new consultant at the same hospital and was incandescent with rage. She also told me that she had forwarded a letter for an appointment at the same clinic the morning before the one with his hospital colleague – cancelling hers in his stride. But the feisty Patricia, fresh from a call from our young grass, swiftly put Mr B in his place, while, at the same time, assuring her pal Sandy that I would be safely delivered into her tender care as planned. Having reached the pinnacle of tolerance and endurance, I appealed to the authorities to put an end to the ludicrous house arrest surveillance which had totally spiralled out of control. It worked. Within a week, I was left alone to deal with my cancer problem, while Dr A and Mr B were never seen or heard of again. I celebrated by spending the beautiful white Christmas of 2010 by the River Thames, singing my heart out at the glorious carol service at St George's Chapel, Windsor, with Elton John and his baby son in the front row. As my *annus horribilis* drew to an end, I gave thanks for surviving my ordeal and braced myself to face a healthier and brighter one in 2011.

That spring, while I was waiting for the new drug to do its job, I went to see my old friends in Norwich, where I had lived for three years on my return to the UK from abroad. As I passed through all the pretty villages and familiar places after landing at Stansted Airport, vivid memories came flooding back of the numerous trips I so enjoyed when I travelled up and down to London from that gorgeous city. With the cherry blossom in bloom, one could not have wished for a more relaxing holiday than to revisit old friends and neighbours still living there, including the premises of Elkins, the wonderful people who published my first book and established me as a writer. Apart from its proximity to the famous Broads and its windmills, what I particularly love about Norfolk is its beautiful churches and Norwich's magnificent cathedral. My visit happened to coincide with the annual Norwich Arts Festival, which hosts the most prodigious talent; so, on hearing strains of the Fauré *Requiem* coming out of one of these churches, my friend and I were lured in, where we were offered a glass of wine, before continuing our way to dinner. Not only did this blissful time afford me space to regroup but also to forget that I had cancer. The fact that my friends had been so relieved that my previous diagnosis was a mistake left me no option but to leave them in blissful ignorance. I continued to use this tactic throughout my treatment, as – in my case – witnessing the distress of loved ones makes it even harder to bear.

By the time I went for my assessment appointment in July, I was so well that I was convinced that the trial drug had done its job, as any sign of a lump had disappeared. Unfortunately, it hadn't quite produced the miraculous effect that I had hoped for. When Sandy offered me the choice of surgery or permanently taking a more potent drug which would have to be monitored every six months, I chose the surgery. Ironically, everyone in the room congratulated me, for not only did it mean that I could get on with the rest of my life and career, but by choosing this option I had proved that I was mentally capable of making a decision to have an operation for breast cancer.

At last, I was able to convince those who doubted me that both Dr A and Mr B had made gross errors of judgement. Once we had all calmed down, including the extraordinary nurse who had been with me from the beginning, Sandy produced the trump card: 'Would next Thursday suit you? I have a free space and can fit you in then.' Within three hours, these wonderful young women had completed all the necessary pre-operative tests so that I would be spared more unnecessary return trips before my operation. After fourteen months' delay, I was finally operated on for a lumpectomy a week later; the following day I was discharged, and the day after that I walked down the main street to do my weekend shopping, as if nothing had happened.

A month later, I returned to have a smaller operation to complete the job before being referred to one of Belfast's main hospitals for an intense course of radiotherapy. The accommodation and crowded conditions in an overstretched hospital might have lacked the luxury enjoyed by those who can afford private care, but I doubt if I could have received better medical attention or personal care than that offered by a much-maligned NHS. Throughout all this upheaval I was concerned that I might not be able to honour a long-standing invitation from Peregrine Butler-Yeats to give a talk to the Probus Club, of which he was president – but I made it, just in time. To say that I was taken by surprise is an understatement, after I faced a room packed to the rafters with men – many of whom were my friends' husbands. Most of these gentlemen were retired or semi-retired businessmen and professionals who met once a month in the local golf club to keep their minds alert, as well as meeting regularly in coffee bars. Concerned that these gentlemen might find a lecture on a local's rather unusual lifestyle a little heavy, I paused to give them a breather and enquire if anyone would like to ask a question. One of these gentlemen, whose wife just happened to be one of my friends, set the ball rolling when he asked me: 'Have you ever had your bottom pinched by an Italian man?' The rest of my seriously planned morning dissolved into an informal chat show about the Italian male species who, I informed them, were perfect gentlemen, so devoted to their families that their eyes would have had little time to stray elsewhere; it was, after all, a men's club I was entertaining, not a class of music students. To have been able to fulfil my long-time promise to Peregrine to talk to his friends gave me the greatest pleasure – for, if it hadn't been for his medical skill and friendship, I wouldn't have made such a wonderful recovery as 'The Reborn Diva'. That remained a secret between us until he sadly passed away the following year.

Positive thinking and creating goals to be achieved are vital ingredients to those recovering from breast cancer – but then, I was enormously privileged through my work and social contacts to have met people in high places to guide me in the right direction. Others to whom I have spoken and who are not so lucky are delighted that I am addressing this delicate issue. In 2012 I was able to spend yet another Christmas by the Thames – which had overflowed, covering the surrounding countryside in so much water that wellington boots were out in force. But what made the trip so special that year was attending morning service at St George's Chapel on Christmas Day, when the choir sang music composed by the late Herbert Howells, with whom I had studied at the Royal College of Music, as well as the Dean remembering the centenary of the *Titanic*, which had been built in my own native city of Belfast. As yet another year drew to a close, it seemed to me that this bringing together of past and present had been sent to pave the way for the return to the life I thought I had lost for ever and the triumphant grand finale which was to follow.

With my friend Luciana Abbado Pestalozza at the Biennale in Venice.

On holiday in Sicily with Susie Park Donatoni, before she
gave me the accidental makeover.

Dr Malcom as best man at my sister's wedding.

The Leone d'Argento (Marco, the Lion King).

*La Wright. Una cantante fuori dal commune*
in a book shop in Venice.

Performing for the Vienna Radio.

West's favourite deer at Ebberston.
Picture reproduced by kind permission of the *Gazette & Herald*.

# Act III

# Scene 7
# Grand Finale

As I became reacquainted with the world around me I was able to reflect on the remarkable changes towards peace and reconciliation which had evolved since my return to Northern Ireland, following the Downing Street agreement in 1993. It was a courageous step negotiated by the eventual Nobel Prize winner John Hume to unite the then British prime minister and his Irish counterpart, Albert Reynolds, in a bid to end so many years of bitter conflict in the six counties of Ireland. On the way back to Dublin that evening the eight members of the delegation from the Irish government allegedly expressed the opinion that only a miracle would bring peace to the north. Five years later that miracle came to pass, after great sacrifices were made by all sides of the divide (as well as the Dublin government) at the signing of The Good Friday Agreement, which gradually restored the province to the prosperous and affluent state it is in today. Its courageous people have been an inspiration to me throughout my own eight years of despair, which paled in significance compared to their thirty, during which they never lost their black sense of humour.

My altruistic hopes of bringing reconciliation through peace as the Mother Teresa of music failed as courage was needed by visiting artistes to ignore world headlines and brave the elements; but those who did were given a warm welcome in spite of the war. It became part of one's daily routine to be searched on entering a city store, as it was when a quick exit had to be made onto the streets if a bomb exploded nearby. The artistic life continued to flourish in the same fashion with audiences remaining seated in cinemas and concert halls, while the show went on regardless. For those who didn't wish to take such risks families and friends would continue to make music at home, while the standard of education soared to today's colossal level, as students had no other option but to stay at home and study. As an international singer I have been privileged to perform in countries where I have worked with, and still do, and become lifelong friends with wonderful people who have shown me the genuine hospitality of their native land, as well as the joy in attempting to communicate in each other's native tongue. But there is always that culture between north and south which seldom bonds, leaving a huge divide and lack of communication between those who live there; but this is not so in Ireland where political issues may inhibit yet do not prevent the constant flow of traffic between Northern Ireland and the Republic. As long as I can remember – which is a long time – culture, fashion and sport have dominated and influenced Irish life, which I thought was normal until interesting people whom I met on my global adventure made me aware of the skills which Ireland has handed out on a plate to those willing to benefit from such God-given opportunities. Even my friends and colleagues, like James Galway and the legendary Derek Bell from the Chieftains to name but a few are forced to stop and reflect at the musical advantages which gave us such unique opportunities on the world stage.

Since my mother was a keen golfer, my father a football and boxing fanatic and yours truly a tennis buff, sport and music were not only an integral part of our lives, but enjoyed as a unit throughout the island of Ireland. The Irish Rugby Union even provided those northerners who are too shy to join in the singing of the Irish national anthem with a rousing song of their own, enabling them to show off their broad northern vowel sounds at the beginning of international matches. Trips to Dublin and Belfast attract both young and old to the latest shows, with stop-offs at border towns along the way to replenish the southerners' food cupboards with less expensive food and booze; the northerners, on the other hand, fill up their cars with cheaper diesel, before heading home over the no longer existing border. An Irish priority which has remained with me throughout my life is the respect for the dead. I could write a book in itself about Irish wakes which turn into parties; yet behind all the craic and shenanigans there is genuine grief and sorrow, which is also accorded to those who although they may have transgressed in life, are forgiven in death.

I didn't have to look further than my own aunt to find what is known locally as a 'professional mourner', who cried at the very sight of a funeral procession without having met or known the deceased. She frequently envisaged her own funeral with the Wright clan out in full force following her coffin down a steep lane from the farm where, as a young widow, she reared and educated her three children. Aunt Rebecca, considerably older than my father, thoroughly spoilt and adored her baby brother who, like myself, was an unexpected late arrival in his generation. Since they remained close throughout their lives, she was also a great influence in mine, too, after I became my father's shadow. My aunt's isolated farm in the lush green countryside of County Tyrone was on top of a hill, with the only adjoining farm for miles around at the top of the long lane leading up from the main road. It was there that I fell in love with nature, animals and the freedom to roam the hills at will. Being the baby sister they never had I enjoyed what was to be a lifetime of being spoiled by my many male cousins, from the age of being taken for rides on tractors and milk cans to being escorted to country dances as a young girl. My aunt also fed me with her wonderful meals of home-produced food which she herself had farmed with her bare hands.

But it was on Sundays and great occasions that she, like my grandmother, left the kitchen and animal-feeding chores to put on her finery for all to see. Swathed in fur, she would swan into church before being escorted to the top pew, which had been reserved for her late husband's family long before she was even thought of. I am often teased about the manner in which I swan off and on the stage, leaving the impression that I am very posh and proud, while my family compare my grand entrances to 'Marge just taking after Aunt Rebecca'! True to tradition, it was the financial gains that Irish soil produced that enabled my aunt to send her son to a grammar school in Yeats's birthplace of Sligo, where he followed in the footsteps of other family clergymen who were educated there, as well as David Wright, my second cousin, who managed to become personal secretary to Lloyd George, the British Liberal prime minister, even though he himself was a labour supporter.

When I received an unexpected email from Cambridge Media informing me that they had taken over Janus Publishing after the death of Sandy Leung, I concluded that one cannot trespass from the path which destiny has paved for one. Not only had a rainbow appeared at the end of the tunnel but, apart from inheriting *The Rise and Fall of a La Scala Diva* they were willing to publish the English edition of *La Diva Rinata*, which would truly transform me into a 'reborn one'. Easter has always brought me great luck and joy as a writer and so, having transmitted the first two chapters of my latest adventure to them, I set off for Cambridge the following spring to sign an agreement for the book, which – by the way – I hope you are enjoying, nearly twenty-five years after signing a similar one for my first baby, *How To Be A Bad Singer!*

Although I was no stranger to Oxbridge, having taken part in several concerts in Oxford's Sheldonian Theatre and Cambridge's Trinity Hall, they were brief visits which left little time between rehearsals and concerts to explore and absorb the atmosphere of these academic gems. Being a writer afforded me more time to get to know the colleges where generations of my family had studied – and still do; indeed, as I write this book my great-nephew is following in his great-grandfather's footsteps by playing football for Trinity College. To imagine that I myself would have a book published in such distinguished surroundings was like a dream come true.

Once we had completed our business I left for home after lunching with my publisher and his lovely Finnish wife in a beautiful hotel overlooking the River Cam and Cambridge's distinctive weeping willow trees; only then did I realise that, by means of writing and technology, I had been given a priceless opportunity to share legendary characters, who had brought me both joy and heartbreak, with those whose lives might be enriched by what I had learnt from knowing them. As I joined the queues of exhausted people at Stansted Airport filing through security checkpoints to reach their Easter holiday destinations, I knew that I had finally emerged from the depths of despair to begin life afresh. And I was right. No sooner had I unpacked my case than I was off to Rome to revisit the city where it all began a long time ago.

Looking back, I must have been out of my mind to attempt such a trip in the June heat less than two years after completing a course of debilitating treatment for breast cancer, but since I had already had to refuse an invitation to a book launch in Milan about the influence that religion had on Puccini's music I certainly wasn't going to refuse one to celebrate the centenary of Benjamin Britten's birth, at Rome Opera's production of his opera *Curlew River* in the splendid basilica of Santa Maria in Ara Coeli.

Other than their own legends like Verdi and Puccini, to name but a few, Britten's music must be revered and performed more frequently in Italy than any other foreign composer that I know of. For instance, when I was invited to join the production team of *The Rape of Lucretia* for Teatro Carlo Fenice in Genoa, his *Death in Venice* was already being performed to full houses in the main theatre as we rehearsed, while many moons before, I myself signed a contract to sing the role of the governess in *The Turn of the Screw* at the old Teatro Margherita. And so, even when my companion for the evening reminded me of the many steps we would have to climb to reach this magnificent church at the highest summit of the Capitoline Hill, I was even more determined to retrace the ones up which I had once conducted so many tourists as an illegal guide.

Gazing at the size and grandeur of Rome's ancient church brought back memories of the first time I was properly introduced to Britten's style of writing when, as a member of the Ambrosian Singers, I sang at the world premiere of his *War Requiem* at the opening of the new Coventry Cathedral. It was a night to remember as this wonderful work of reconciliation was performed at the highest level, overlooking the ruins of the old cathedral, which had been destroyed during the Second World War on a night of fierce bombing on Coventry. I am ashamed to say that until that evening I had considered Britten's music to be an acquired taste, but once I became acclimatised to his unique harmonies and haunting themes I was, like the Italians, hooked for life. Nevertheless, I wondered what the great man himself would have thought of the more modern production in which the Madwoman runs around wheeling a trolley from the nearest supermarket: It seemed so far removed from the memories that I cherish of all the wonderful concerts and recordings that I took part in back in England with Ben and his partner, the immaculate Peter Pears, for whom *Curlew River* was originally written.

By sheer coincidence, it was my first visit to Rome since 2005, which happened to coincide with the arrival of cardinals and dignitaries from all over the world to elect a new pope, Pope Benedict XVI, whose retirement in 2013, just before my visit, once again focused world attention on the chimney of the Vatican's Sistine Chapel to watch for the white smoke billowing out to announce his successor, Pope Francis. But what saddened me was the decline in the economy that had hit Italy in the intervening years, like so many other eurozone countries. The streets, once so full of night life and prosperity, were almost deserted, except for tourists. When I asked a taxi driver why there was such an uncanny silence he explained that many residents could not afford their car insurance, let alone the petrol to keep them on the road. Restaurants and bars, once so full of people, were quite empty in comparison to when I lived in Rome in the affluent era of the *dolce vita* of wine, women and song. With severe government cuts to the once well-funded arts, concerts were restricted, leaving artistes out of work and having to seek employment elsewhere or by other means. It made me realise that I had made the right decision to return to the more financially secure safety of my native land, or I would have found myself in the same financial dilemma as those colleagues I had left behind in Italy. Yet there was much to celebrate when I caught up with my long-term agent and friend Ornella Cogliolo, as we celebrated my being awarded the prestigious Leone d'Argento in which our wonderful working relationship had played such a major role. How we reminisced about the distinguished people who over so many years had remained loyal to us and contributed so much to my books. They are all given special mention in both *La Wright. Una cantante fouri dal commune* and *The Reborn Diva*, which is soon to be translated into its Italian title, *La Diva Rinata*.

Over luncheon with an old friend in the beautiful Piazza Navona we talked so much about the past that I decided to remain there after she had gone and live for the present in this wonderful square where I had spent so much of my time when I was living in Rome, taking tourists round its statues and fountains. Italians are so appreciative of one's effort to speak their language that I decided to brush up my Italian and express myself in that idioms of idioms, much to the delight of the waiters who gave me 'Diva attention' after I unashamedly informed them that I was a *cantante lirica*. Italians just love opera singers and treat them like royalty, much to my embarrassment, but on that balmy summer day in Rome, where the seeds of civilisation were sewn in 783 BC, I realised that the time had arrived to bid farewell to the past and move on to pastures new with fresh vision and hope. So many of my generation of musicians and artistes had either died or moved to more tranquil surroundings to enjoy their twilight years in anonymity, away from the behind-the-scenes stress that is unavoidable when they become a public figure for the sake of their art.

Yet, I was determined not to be sad and to say farewell to Rome in style by hiring a car on the morning of my departure to take me round the places which had brought me such luck, success and happiness. As I pointed out landmarks to the driver along the way I relived the magic of getting my big break at the Accademia of Santa Cecilia when I sang the 'St Luke Passion' by the Polish composer Kristof Penderecki; the Spanish Steps where I had taken so many tourists during my illegal days as a guide, and the Piazza del Popolo, where I would gather for an ice cream with other extras after filming with the great American film director William Wilder. As we passed the Vatican I asked the driver to slow down so I could absorb the moment of history being made inside the Sistine Chapel where the cardinals had just gathered to elect the new pope. Then it was full steam ahead to the airport where, over the years, I had caught so many planes to unknown destinations either to sing or answer an emergency call from an artiste in distress.

I was over the moon when friends invited me to their wonderful hotel's eighteenth birthday party overlooking Carlingford Lough and the Mountains of Mourne; not only did I look forward to the craic but the scrumptious food for which it is well known. Since I had provided the entertainment at the original opening of the hotel I thought I would surprise them by bringing along one or two of the Gershwin melodies I sang that evening, even though, according to statistics, I was long past my sell-by date. Having eaten from a buffet which would have graced any state occasion, I was just about to spring my surprise act on the assembled guests when, lo and behold, the chef emerged from the kitchen and began to make his way round the room impersonating an Italian tenor with one of the finest voices I have ever heard, accompanied by an equally fine orchestra on a backing track. Suddenly, he made his way towards me and sat down on my lap to personally serenade me with this wonderful tenor voice, which belonged to him and no one else. In real life he comes from Belfast and gives classical recitals as well as these wonderful operatic appearances as a singing chef with his soprano 'waitress'. Realising that there was no way I could compete after that I decided to bow out and leave it to the new generation, alive with energy and a modern technique which demanded young muscles. But it was not all over: for a year later I was back in Italy making a video with a famous bass colleague from the past.

Five traumatic years passed before I was able to accept Renzo Stevanato's invitation to sing 'La ci darem la mano', the duet from Mozart's *Don Giovanni* between Don Giovanni and the servant girl Zerlina. That evening in Venice when I was presented with the Leone d'Argento life achievement award seemed but a dream, for it was that same night that I discovered the lump on my breast; so when I received an invitation to Venice at the end of November in 2014 to attend *La Notte D'Oro* for recipients of the Leone d'Oro (Marco's sibling) at the famous Lido del Cinema I was determined to accept this challenge, not only to show my appreciation of the wonderful honour bestowed on me in 2009, but to get back into vocal training to fulfil my promise to Renzo, even if I was rather long in the tooth to be a sweet servant girl. But before I set off for this idyllic paradise I wanted to relive that momentous occasion with my friend Margaret de Wend Fenton who, with her daughter Clarissa, made the journey all the way from their home in Ebberston Hall in Yorkshire to share those unforgettable days with me in Venice.

# Scene 8

# Encore

I first fell in love with Ebberston Hall and Yorkshire when Margaret and West invited me to sing at their son's wedding in the quaint church on the edge of their estate. Margaret was one of the numerous friends from that part of the world whom I met soon after my return to a London still buzzing with excitement after the wedding of Prince Charles and Lady Diana Spencer. As I made my way by train from Kings Cross to York and beyond, I understood why my mother had fallen in love with Yorkshire and its warm-hearted people during her teaching years in Doncaster. But Ebberston was something else – a relatively small Palladian mansion near Scarborough, described by Hugh Montgomery Massingberd in his article in *Time Magazine* as the smallest Tom Thumb estate in England. You can imagine my delight when a year after Johnny and Jane's wedding Margaret and West invited me to look after the hall and visiting tourists while they dashed off to Romania to help those suffering hardship under the brutal dictatorship of Nicolae Ceausescu.

The De Wend Fentons passed on their passion for adventure and discovering how other people lived to their children, who have been left with wonderful memories of the countries they all explored together. Before he married, West went off to join the Foreign Legion, from which he was rescued by a bridesmaid from their eventual society wedding at St Margaret's, Westminster. A book called *The Reluctant*

*Legionnaire,* giving an account of West's extraordinary adventure, was only one of so many stories which those who knew this flamboyant character cherish. And so, along with his family and friends, I would like to share the West that we all loved with those who never had the privilege to know him like we did.

As a passionate animal lover I couldn't wait to spend a month amongst the animals which West loved and embraced as they grazed or roamed around the estate; but it wasn't long before I discovered that once others encroached on their territory the boot was on the other foot. The white-and-black geese ignored me during the day but at night I used to marvel at the way they made their way as a flock to the pond into which water from the moors cascaded in the form of a magnificent fountain.

The Chinese geese were extremely hostile to visitors and were likely to bite those who even attempted to be friendly, while the proud and beautiful peacocks ignored those with whom they were unacquainted, as did the wonderful llama who grazed alongside the Shetland ponies in the field looking out over the wondrous Yorkshire wolds. But the turkey to which West was particularly attached did not appreciate being abandoned in preference to a trip to Romania and perched himself on top of a railing outside the front door of the hall, where he lay in wait so that he could chase me out through the main gates onto the road. To West his name was Henry, but to those who were not so fond of him he was called Paxo, after a packet of stuffing. He eventually escaped from being carved up at the Christmas dinner table after he was sent off to stud to breed lots more festive fare.

Surely there must be no more magnificent sight than a stag gazing down from the top of a hill. I had never been in close contact with a herd of deer until I was introduced to them at Ebberston where I would watch them grazing in their special field on the estate beside the church. West was totally devoted to his deer – reminding me of Emily Brontë's Heathcliffe, straight out of *Wuthering Heights* – as he strode down from the moors to his herd in the field where he himself now rests. To give the reader an idea of the sheer beauty of this spot – looking down on the cottage where the poet Wordsworth spent the night before his wedding – I have especially chosen a photo of a white hart posing near West's grave beneath the lovely church where my one-woman show made its debut.

When funds were urgently needed to restore the hall to its former glory I offered to give a recital in the village church to promote this worthy cause. Realising that entrepreneurial skills were needed to entice punters, Margaret and I decided that the nearest town of Scarborough, whose greatest contribution to the world of literature was the famous playwright Alan Ayckbourn, was the ideal location from which to promote the concert: and so, armed with posters and publicity from the local press that a 'Scala Diva' was about to give a recital in the Ebberston village church, Margaret and I set off for Scarborough to lure music lovers to an evening of Wagner, Mahler, negro spirituals and Irish folk songs, followed by a candlelight supper at the hall. Since recitals can be forbidding and attended exclusively by elitists I decided to call it 'Music for Everyone' so that all tastes would be catered for.

What we didn't cater for was the sudden disappearance of the piano accompanist, leaving me to 'face the music' on my own. My colleagues have always been intrigued and entertained by my unique style of piano playing which, to their elitist and conventional taste, resembles Liberace more than Lang Lang. Ever since my piano teacher turned my life upside-down by informing me that my hands were too small for me to be a concert pianist, I developed my own inhibited way round the keyboard. No longer restricted to following the written note, I was able to keep my fingers nimble by familiarising myself with the piano parts of works I was studying, as well as unashamedly giving them a 'Marge makeover' if I felt that my accompaniment was easier on the ear than Wagner's.

With only a day left until a posh recital, which was fast turning into a comedy act, there was no other option but to play for myself. As if appearing in public as a pianist for the first time was not enough I had no piano to play on! Only West could have saved the situation by coming up with a brilliant idea: before we could say 'Jack Robinson' Margaret and I were ordered into the car before he drove us to the beautiful city of York, where we hired a wonderful keyboard from their top music store. As well as an authentic-sounding piano, I had a choice of other instruments to choose from which made the evening so much more interesting than listening to voice and piano for over an hour and a half. Playing to a full house, we placed the keyboard where, sitting down, I was able to embrace the audience and entertain them with stories, before we all met up for supper at the hall at the end of a perfect summer evening. It certainly was a night to remember and one which – for me – introduced classical music to real everyday people.

Reminiscing and being with old friends again, with whom I had shared so much, was to be the prelude to my trip to Venice when, five weeks later, the glorious Grand Finale to my story ended a long 'pregnancy', before I finally gave birth to a new and wonderful beginning.

The weeks between my return to Ireland from Yorkshire and my departure for Venice were filled with excitement, exaltation and wild anticipation as I prepared to embark on the greatest adventure of my life. Without doubt, Venice may be the city of love and romance, but I am going to take you on a trip of a lifetime to this wondrous paradise of culture and art that you will not find online.

Before we take off I must advise those on board to pack wellingtons, umbrellas, walking sticks and pills for those prone to rheumatism and arthritis, because it is winter in Venice, when serenading gondoliers, although ever present, need to protect their voices, as indeed do I when I perform there.

I have never been to Venice at the height of the tourist season because opera houses in Italy don't officially open in winter until December, while the Biennale contemporary music festival, to which I was a frequent visitor, took place in the autumn, just as the weather changed after the intense heat of summer. Nevertheless, when the sun reveals Venice in all its seasonal splendour, it is a never-to-be-forgotten sight to behold.

I shall never forget an epic train journey I made from Milan to Venice in the month of November to begin rehearsals for the modern opera with which I was to open the season one December. As I made my way up the platform towards my second-class compartment a soprano colleague, also en route to Teatro La Fenice, graciously waved from her first-class one. Since we had to pay our expenses from our own pockets before being paid, I saw no point in travelling as a diva, especially as there would be no reception committee at the station to receive us. As we drew out of Milan we ran into bad weather which got worse as we got near Lake Garda and Verona, scene of the wonderful open-air summer opera season which attracts tourists from all over the world. Suddenly, the train stopped in its tracks after a sudden flash of lightning followed by thunder and torrential rain made it impossible to continue further. Finally, after a two-hour delay, we arrived at a deserted Venice railway station around 9 o'clock in the evening, from where we caught a water bus to St Mark's Square – the nearest stop to our hotel.

Never in our wildest dreams could we have imagined the scene that greeted us as we made our way into the square in search of a porter: the torrential downpours had caused the waters from the lagoon to rise so high that planks had to be built over the flooded square to enable people to walk. Because Venice is built on a number of islands and canals, no cars are allowed around St Mark's Island, leaving walking and boats as the only means of transport. Just when were about to burst into real operatic tears wonderful porters rushed towards us and carried us, shoulder high, to a trolley on to which they loaded our diva luggage, with my internationally renowned colleague and me perched on top of it. It usually takes about fifteen minutes to walk from St Mark's Square through the maze of narrow alleys and bridges to the quaint Hotel Taverna La Fenice, from where the hotel staff were about to send out a distress signal – just as we were making our way through the maze of narrow alleys, where every sound echoes in the dead of night. Suddenly, a receptionist whom I knew well from many visits there said, 'They're coming; I can hear Marjorie laughing her head off.' It was acclaimed as an opera within an opera. Never before had Teatro La Fenice seen two prima donnas arrive to open the season perched on top of a baggage trolley along with their finery.

Once I had booked my hotel and flight to Venice I devoted my time to getting myself into shape, both physically and vocally. Every day I exercised going up and down stairs in preparation for the many bridges I would have to cross, as hailing a taxi where no cars were allowed wasn't a possibility. Always a keen walker, I strolled every day in the autumn sunshine, as I knew I would have to negotiate my way through once familiar alleys, now crowded with tourists taking advantage of cheap flights which were not available in the Venice I knew so long ago. Then, one could go for an evening stroll in winter without meeting a soul, stopping off for a bite in a cosy trattoria along the way, completely void of tourists. Although my voice was still intact after breast cancer I wasn't sure if I could measure up to the professional standard required to sing Mozart's famous duet 'La ci darem la mano' for bass and soprano; and so I had to revert to the technique demanding athlete's training which not only had steered me through so many vocal adventures over the years but was bringing me back to full strength after radium treatment; it was as if I was slowly but surely gaining a new lease of life which I intended to let loose and prove the doctors wrong. By the end of November 2015 I felt I was fit enough to race in the Olympics, as I set off to be reborn as a singer in the city which had lovingly embraced me as an artiste back in the good old days.

Dawn was breaking over the Dublin mountains as I made my way into the impressive Aer Lingus terminal. Because it was winter there was no through flight to Venice to coincide with my dates, so that I had to fly to London Gatwick before catching a connecting British Airways flight to Venice's Marco Polo airport. It wasn't until the girl at the check-in desk nearly swooned over my ticket at the very thought of flying to such a romantic destination that I realised where I was going. When she discreetly inquired if I would require 'assistance' – meaning a wheelchair – I politely refused, telling her in my diva voice that I was an opera singer, about to make a come-back in Venice. By the time I had walked miles between flight connections, caught two different planes and negotiated my way between two terminals and security checks at Gatwick, I was beginning to regret not accepting her offer. But the fact remained that I had done it, making all those weeks of training, so necessary to sustaining the voice, worthwhile.

My rather unorthodox style of singing is personally derived from hours spent watching golfers and tennis players using their entire bodies to generate the energy and stamina needed to win grand slams and championships. Inspired by their prowess I have proved that movement makes the body breathe, so that by the time I reached passport control at Gatwick's North Terminal I had walked so far and accumulated so much breath that the young man at the barrier asked me if I needed help. 'No thank you,' I replied, 'I am an opera singer on my way to perform in Venice.' He must have thought that, given my advanced years, I was absolutely bonkers. I shiver to imagine what his reaction would have been if I had told him that I was going to sing the part of Zerlina, the sweet servant girl in Mozart's *Don Giovanni*, with one of Italy's most distinguished dons.

A singer's life resembles that of a plane crew who fly to exotic destinations but never have time to explore them. Apart from having to honour a contract restricting one's movements to a heavy rehearsal schedule, rest and restaurants, there is little or no time left for sightseeing, so that the Venice I knew was the tourist attractions around St Mark's Square, the railway station and Teatro La Fenice. And so, when I was invited to the golden night at the famous Lido del Cinema, I couldn't wait to explore what I had missed over the years and be reunited with my friends on the famous Lido, home of the Venice Film Festival, and where *Death in Venice*, based on Thomas Mann's novella and starring Dirk Bogarde, was shot. This poignant piece of writing and its location also inspired Benjamin Britten to write his last opera.

The Venice Lido is the eleven-kilometre stretch of sandbar dividing Venice from the Adriatic Sea, where Venetians love to swim and sunbathe. As the journey involved a turbulent hour's boat ride from the airport to my hotel, it was early evening when I reached the stupendous Hungaria Palace hotel, bringing back memories of the evening when I arrived on a trolley at the Hotel Taverna La Fenice to an equally warm welcome. Perhaps it is because we are all northerners, but I have always shared an exceptionally loving relationship with the true Venetian people, who have a sense of humour to die for – rather like the black humour which steered Northern Ireland through the Troubles, while personally landing me in deep waters with those who are bereft of this blessed gift: indeed it served us well in gathering up the pieces after 'unforeseen circumstances' forced the last-minute cancellation of the three nights of glory planned for the Lido del Cinema. Although I was bitterly disappointed for my colleagues, I relished the opportunity to spend more time alone with them and to rehearse my duet with my bass colleague who had, until my arrival, been very secretive and elusive about the date and place of the performance: the only information

I could extract from him was that he would give it worldwide publicity. But this was Italy, where so many 'unforeseen circumstances' had disrupted performances in which I had been due to take part that I was well used to last-minute changes of plans. Without fail, they were either resolved or replaced with bonuses – like an unforgettable evening in Naples when the car in which the conductor and I were travelling was stopped outside radio headquarters by a group of angry metal mechanics, including the engineers due to record our concert. After fighting our way through the masses, we finally reached our venue where the angry audience were about to disperse, leaving behind one member who had come to welcome his Hungarian conductor friend and colleague to Naples. When we discovered that those in charge had already departed before our arrival to avoid discussing the delicate matter of payment and reimbursement, our knight in shining armour rose to the occasion by taking me along with the conductor to a magnificent restaurant, where he wined and dined us overlooking the bay of Naples. At the end of the evening our host begged us to delay our return to Rome so that we could accept an invitation to the royal luncheon he was holding in honour of his cousin's wife, the Duchess of Aosta, daughter of the then French pretender, the Comte du Paris. My Hungarian colleague was sure that his ducal friend was just being polite, but I assured him that it was sincere: I was so glad I managed to persuade him to accept the invitation, as the duke's monarchist friends couldn't wait to meet the abandoned conductor and prima donna whom their royal host had rescued from the previous night's shenanigans.

To return to Venice, I had hardly unpacked my suitcase when Don Giovanni, aka Renzo Stevanato, arranged to meet me near the Rialto Bridge with Billy, his adored and beautifully groomed white Maltese dog, from where we made our way to the apartment of the late but never-to-be-forgotten tenor, Mario del Monaco. As we chatted our way up the fifty-three stairs, with Billy leading the way, I was gasping for breath, just as I had done five years earlier when Nicola Catto and I had climbed up and down them on that momentous day in December, when all our dreams were realised in that distinguished environment.

Mario del Monaco's Venetian apartment is maintained like a shrine in honour of the 20th century's greatest tenor. It is from there that

Renzo Stevanato, one of the great maestro's students and disciples, continues to carry on the del Monaco legacy. As well as excelling in the role of Don Giovanni, he is also well known for his interpretation of the doctor in Verdi's *Macbeth*, both of which he has performed with the finest Italian producers and conductors. With so many shared memories, I couldn't wait to make music with such an experienced performer who, like me, was so anxious to give back to future generations what we had both achieved from such a great era.

I hadn't seen a video of the evening that changed my life when I discovered a lump in my breast. As we sat watching it I felt as if I had just been hit by a tornado, for only then did I realise that if I had not taken desperate measures to avoid a mastectomy I wouldn't have been sitting in the home of the world's greatest tenor listening to a replay of the last time I had sung in public; to imagine that I was going to make an after-breast-cancer come-back within the same walls was completely and utterly surreal. As we relived that evening I was left without words when I discovered that the drama surrounding our rehearsal, two hours before the concert, had been overheard by the team of helpers preparing for the after-concert reception in the adjoining room. Renzo also confessed that he had been a silent witness to the drama when Nicola and I had been forced to take the bull by the horns and go for it, without ever having heard each other sing or play; that I had to change into my evening attire in the bathroom without a hairdresser in sight; that I had no option but to plaster make-up on top of what I had already on, while, at the same time, warning Nicola about the tactics I was about to inflict on him. No wonder they were all agog with excitement to see what was about to happen; but once we got going we became so immersed in the beautiful music which we had chosen together that we were oblivious to everyone and everything around us. Having relived those precious moments, Renzo and I arranged to meet up again the following morning at the same venue to employ our own tactics regarding 'La ci darem la mano' (There we will give each other our hands), except that, unknown to me, Don Giovanni, who is also president of the Friends of Mario del Monaco, had devised his own individual production, modelled on the video we had just watched.

After a hearty breakfast fit for Aida, I set off across the lagoon for the forty-minute water-bus journey to the Rialto Bridge, passing so many familiar stops as we sailed up the Grand Canal. For those of you opera lovers who are familiar with Mozart's tragic comedy, Don Giovanni is the rakish seducer who tries to lure beautiful women to his castle, his latest victim to succumb to his charms being the sweet servant girl Zerlina – me – whom he is trying to lure away from her fiancé, Masetto. It was only then that I found out that we were to perform our long-awaited duet before a group of distinguished guests the following day with minimum time to rehearse. And so, when he broke the news that no pianist was available at such short notice, I offered my services, since I was already familiar with the piano accompaniment as well as the bass part. Renzo was delighted, since he had already observed me compose the accompaniment to the luscious Irish folk songs I had sung with the same piano, five years earlier.

At last the appointed hour arrived when a group of stalwart guests from my presentation concert reassembled to applaud my debut as Zerlina, leaving the ever-patient Billy to retire to his bed in the adjoining hall to listen to yet another opera singer invade his privacy and precious time with his master.

Having negotiated my way through the piano introduction, I had just reached the point where Zerlina coyly begins to respond to Don Giovanni's advances, when out of his bed jumped Billy who immediately threw me off my stride by barking his head off. But the show had to go on, and, like the true pros that they were, Don Giovanni and Zerlina finished their love scene with the rake's arms spread around the piano stool, while Billy barked his way through his own chorus lines. Meanwhile, our friends rose to their feet to record the unforgettable scene for posterity on their IPads.

It turned out that our long-awaited duet was just the overture to the presentation of a magnificently embossed certificate declaring that I was one of a hundred world figures chosen to represent their countries in Venetia Free Culture, an exclusive organisation which had been formed to bring goodwill and non-partisan opportunities to Venice and the Veneto region. In my opinion, representing one's country is everyone's dream, but to be chosen to unite Irish and Venetian culture is one from which I never want to wake up. That evening we raised a glass to those who had made this all possible: to my mother, who gave birth to me in Belfast; to both my parents who brought me up in a cross-border culture embracing both sides of the divide; and to my paternal grandmother, who introduced her extraordinary talents to a conservative and tone-deaf clan of Wrights.

I was privileged to have been born into a home where my loving and talented parents showered me with cultural gifts. My father, who had a beautiful lyrical tenor voice, was a member of a well-known male-voice choir, while my mother was a contralto of considerable teaching experience who took great pride in the male voice quartet she coached on Friday nights while I did my English homework.

My father was second tenor, while a promising young man with a more velvet tone was on the top line. And so, at an early age, I was introduced to controlled, immaculately trained tenor voices, both as a classical concert singer and as a member of the acclaimed Ambrosian Singers, until I went to live in Italy in the late 1960s, where I was to spend the remaining years of my career working alongside tenor voices of a very different calibre.

To begin with, male Italian opera singers are a 'package deal': they have the looks, God-given voices, a beautiful language with which to express their emotions, and the muscular power to blast off their glorious music to the rafters and beyond – like a missile en route to its target.

As a member of the Ambrosian Singers, I had the enormous good fortune to take part in the many famous operatic recordings for which our never-to-be-forgotten director John McCarthy required our services. We became so used to working with famous conductors and artistes that, as hard-boiled professional musicians, we just did our job with complete nonchalance; but when the elegant and suave Italian conductor Carlo Mario Giulini escorted his compatriot tenor Franco Corelli into the recording studio we girls nearly forgot to sing!! Not only was he devastatingly good looking but he possessed top notes the like of which we had never heard in our singing lives.

As a soprano used to singing demanding top notes, I empathised with tenors in case they might miss exposed top notes which those out front have paid huge prices to hear – as in Donezzetti's *Daughter of the Regiment* where the poor tenor has to hit one top C after another. In one famous Italian opera house they have a claque up in the Gods waiting to boo if a tenor misses them; once he has given them what they want he is cheered on his way.

In my eyes, one of the greatest vocal technicians was Luciano Pavarotti, possibly because he had been a choirboy, singing duets with his father, before becoming a well-known teacher. He had all the tricks of vocal technique at his fingertips and never missed a note, because he knew exactly where he was going. As he grew older, when most singers would have retired – because age takes its toll on tired muscles – he knew how to cut corners. I learnt so much from watching him sing Puccini's 'Nessun Dorma' that I applied the timing of his top notes to my own voice with considerable success! But the king of tenors in Italy in the mid 1920s was the never-ever-to-be-forgotten Mario del Monaco who played a principal role in my own life when, ninety six years after his death, I was awarded the prestigious Leone d'Argento lifetime achievement award by the Fondazione Internazionale Mario del Monaco.

By the time my own career had taken off in Italy in the seventies, Mario del Monaco no longer sang principal roles at the Metropolitan Opera in New York, or in Europe where he had been a megastar for so many years; nevertheless, his virile presence and swarthy good looks, along with the passion and strength of vocal sound which he exuded, made him King of Kings.

His 100th birthday on 27 July 2015 not only ignited a centenary year of festivities in his honour, organised by a group of distinguished Venetian artistes and musicians who lovingly preserve the legendary talent which del Monaco left behind, but global plans to bring back the golden era of the glittering Gondola D'Oro Light Music Festival, and Marco's sibling, the Famous Leone d'Oro.

I hope that my story will teach other artistes and people everywhere never to give up hope – as there is always a light which eternally burns at the end of the tunnel.